Guiding School Improvement with

action Research

Richard Sagor

Association for Supervision
and Curriculum Development
Alexandria, Virginia USA

Association for Supervision and Curriculum Development
1703 N. Beauregard St. • Alexandria, VA 22311-1714 USA
Telephone: 1-800-933-2723 or 703-578-9600 • Fax: 703-575-5400
Web site: http://www.ascd.org • E-mail: member@ascd.org

Printed in the United States of America.

May 2000 member book (p). ASCD Premium, Comprehensive, and Regular members periodically receive ASCD books as part of their membership benefits. No. FY00-07.

ASCD Stock No. 100047
ASCD member price: $20.95   nonmember price: $24.95

Library of Congress Cataloging-in-Publication Data
Sagor, Richard.
    Guiding school improvement with action research / Richard Sagor.
        p. cm.
Includes bibliographical references and index.
"ASCD stock no. 100047"—T.p. verso.
    ISBN 0-87120-375-8
    1. Action research in education—United States—Methodology. 2.
School improvement programs—United States.   I. Title.
    LB1028.24 .S34 2000
    371.2'07'0973—dc21   00-008206

05   04   03   02   01   00   10 9 8 7 6 5 4 3 2 1

Dedicated to the memory of my beloved father and friend,
Irving Sagor
1917–1999

Guiding School Improvement with Action Research

Preface

Charles Dickens begins A *Tale of Two Cities* **asserting, "It was the** best of times, it was the worst of times." Those words ring in my ears when I reflect on recent visits I have made to schools across North America.

Occasionally I visit a school that makes me want to go back and relive my childhood. The unbridled joy of the children and the excitement they experience while learning seems impossible to beat. Furthermore, the professional satisfaction being derived by the teachers comes mighty close to matching the joy of the kids. In these schools I see curious and successful teachers vitally involved in their professional work and in the learning of their students. It is no surprise that these educators are happy and mentally healthy adults. I enviously look and listen as these teachers collaborate, introduce novel strategies, and assess individual and classroom progress, then change strategies based upon the results. Not surprisingly, the hallways and classroom walls are filled with evidence of the consequences of teacher work and student learning.

Unfortunately, I often visit other schools where even the air seems heavy. Students and teachers continuously watch the clock. Students count the days until school is out, and teachers count the years until retirement. Education is something that is endured, not treasured. When I listen to teacher talk at these schools, I hear explanations about why things aren't as they should be: the community doesn't support education, the parents have the wrong values, the administration doesn't support teachers, the facilities are inadequate, and so on. The negative thinking isn't limited to the adults. Students in these schools complain, "I can't do that" or "This is too hard" or "Why do we have to do this?" The attitudes of defeatism are so contagious that I begin looking at the clock myself, wishing that it were time to leave!

My research, as well as the published work of others, has convinced me that all schools could (and should) be exciting places in which to learn and fulfilling places in which to teach. More important, it is within our power to bridge the differences between the environments that are exciting and growth orientated and the ones that are characterized by routine and stagnation.

Perhaps it is more than coincidence that we start many children's education off with the famous children's story *The Little Engine That Could*. The message of that story—having the belief that one can prevail (what psychologists call "efficacy")—is the essential ingredient for long-term success and is probably the most salient difference between the faculties at effective and ineffective schools. However, unlike the situation in the children's story, it will take more than chanting "I think I can, I think I can, I think I can!" to get public school educators over their mountain of despair. What is required to change a "defeatist" school into a "hopeful" one is a transformation—a transformation marked by new habits of mind, new forms of collegial interaction, and the creation of a climate and culture that support true professionalism.

Collaborative action research, though not a magical cure for all that ails education, can be a powerful force supporting the transformation from defeatism to an "I think I can" work environment. I know this from my research into the work of teachers such as Deborah Meier and Marva Collins, and of networks such as Carl Glickman's League of Professional Schools, Ted Sizer's Coalition of Essential Schools, and Henry Levin's Accelerated Schools Project; and from the research of scholars such as Judith Warren Little, Milbrey McLaughlin, Ann Lieberman, Susan Rosenholtz, and others. These sources have demonstrated to me the incredible power of teacher and student inquiry. A second basis for my optimism comes from my personal experience. I have experienced the power of inquiry in schools where I have worked, with colleagues I have taught with and in my own classroom. This book builds upon this second source of insight.

I might have titled this book *Tool Time for Educators*. The components of the seven-step action research process that the book explores (finding a focus, clarifying theories, identifying research questions, collecting data, analyzing data, reporting results, and taking action) are nothing more than tools to be used by creative professionals.

Historically, efforts to characterize education debated whether teaching was a purely creative, intuitive, artistic endeavor or an applied science. Both postures have proven inadequate. Ultimately, as any successful teacher knows, education is a wonderful and dynamic mixture of both art and science. Mastery of pedagogical strategy isn't enough to ensure that students will learn and leave school feeling good about themselves. On the other hand, although charismatic teachers may capture the interest of their students, more than mere pizzazz is required to successfully help young people develop important and transferable lifelong skills. The real virtuosity of teaching and the magic of a productive school are realized when mastery of pedagogy is combined with an artistic ability to connect with the learner.

I was recently reminded of this as I helped my 6th grade daughter with a truly creative science project. The teacher wanted her students to understand the operations of simple machines. She asked them to invent a useful product (not yet on the market) and produce a prototype. The invention needed to use several simple machines. Ellisa decided to produce a "Beanie Baby Duster." Her final product was quite remarkable; it looked like a miniature drive-though car wash. The Beanie Baby sat on a seat and was pulled through a gauntlet of swirling feather dusters. Her prototype and her technical write-up demonstrated that she had acquired a clear understanding of the wheel, axle, pulley, and lever. What I gleaned from this was that although "simple machines" weren't very exciting by themselves, the infinite uses that creative people have devised for them demonstrate what marvelous tools they truly are.

This book is about the use of a tool. Like all tools in a teacher's repertoire, it isn't the tool itself that possesses the magic; it is the combination of the science (represented by the tool) and its artistic use by a teacher that produces the great learning experience.

One important characteristic of the simple machines my daughter used with her Beanie Baby Duster, as well as some of the basic hand tools in a home workshop, is their versatility. As you read through this book, you will see that I am infatuated with this particular tool, action research. I am even a little ashamed of my excitement regarding something that, in and of itself, is really no more than an instrument. But as I've reflected on these feelings, I realize that it is the versatility of action research that most appeals to me. Disciplined inquiry and data-based decision making have worked for me when my concern was focused on the problem of a single child and when, as a principal, my concern was the impact of a curriculum on hundreds of young people.

Action research is as helpful to a 1st grade teacher teaching basic language skills as it is to a teacher of high school physics. Furthermore, the seven-step action research process is a productive routine if engaged in by a lone practitioner, a team of colleagues, or an entire faculty seeking to accomplish a schoolwide agenda.

Those realizations presented a problem for me and my editors at ASCD as we prepared this manuscript. Should our focus be the use of this tool by the single teacher? That didn't feel right because it would imply that the action research technology wasn't useful for groups. Ultimately we decided that the volume should deal with all three forums for the conduct of action research—the individual practitioner, the collegial group, and the schoolwide faculty. Parts I, II, and III of the book focus on the use of action research by individual teachers as well as ad hoc teams of colleagues who share similar concerns. The focus in Part IV shifts to the school as the primary unit of change. This section includes examples of how action research can be used to improve a school's culture, help accomplish assessments for evaluation and accreditation, and assist a faculty in the accomplishment of schoolwide goals for student learning.

An additional concern had to do with the examples I would use to illustrate the seven steps of the action research process. One compelling argument was to focus entirely on the acquisition of basic skills. This idea was attractive because the current focus on standards has caused many educators to amplify their focus on the 3 Rs. But looking exclusively at the assessment of basic skills instruction would overlook one of the more powerful aspects of teacher research—its ability to employ a wide range of data to inform our work with nonacademic objectives. For this reason I have used examples of teachers using action research on both academic and affective objectives drawn from the elementary, middle, and high school levels.

Keep in mind that the ideas presented here, like the instruction my daughter received on simple machines, is aimed only at illustrating some possible uses and applications of action research. The examples I provide do not reveal the full power of action research and reflective practice. The magic of data driven, reflective practice is unleashed when you, the practicing educator, artistically apply this process to those issues of teaching and learning that matter to you and that will ultimately enhance the lives of your students.

I know that in the creative hands of teachers and administrators the ideas in this book will produce things I could never have imagined. After all, who would have thought that the tools of the ancients would give rise to the invention of a Beanie Baby Duster?

Finally, I have enjoyed writing this book, which is my part of a "dialogue." As you explore the ideas that follow and others that your own creativity inspires, I would enjoy hearing your voice, your part of the dialogue. I would be delighted and honored to hear and respond to your reactions and ideas. Feel free to write me at the Institute for the Study of Inquiry in Education, or e-mail me with your thoughts, reactions, suggestions, or issues.

Richard Sagor
Institute for the Study of Inquiry in Education
602 NE 3rd Ave., Suite E-174
Camas, WA 98607
E-Mail: rdsagor@isie.org

I.

Action Research:
A Methodology for
Refining Teaching

1   What Is Action Research?

A succinct definition of action research appears in the workshop materials we use at the Institute for the Study of Inquiry in Education. That definition states that action research

> is a disciplined process of inquiry conducted *by* and *for* those taking the action. The primary reason for engaging in action research is to assist the "actor" in improving and/or refining his or her actions.

Practitioners who engage in action research inevitably find it to be an empowering experience. Action research has this positive effect for many reasons. Obviously, the most important is that action research is always relevant to the participants. Relevance is guaranteed because the focus of each research project is determined by the researchers, who are also the primary consumers of the findings.

Perhaps even more important is the fact that action research helps educators be more effective at what they care most about—their teaching and the development of their students. Seeing students grow is probably the greatest joy educators can experience. When teachers have convincing evidence that their work has made a real difference in their students' lives, the countless hours and endless efforts of teaching seem worthwhile.

The Action Research Process

Educational action research can be engaged in by a single teacher, by a group of colleagues who share an interest in a common problem, or by the entire faculty of a school. Whatever the scenario, action research always involves the same seven-step process. These seven steps, which become an endless cycle for the inquiring teacher, are the following:

1. Selecting a focus

3

2. Clarifying theories
3. Identifying research questions
4. Collecting data
5. Analyzing data
6. Reporting results
7. Taking informed action

Step 1—Selecting a Focus

The action research process begins with serious reflection directed toward identifying a topic or topics worthy of a busy teacher's time. Considering the incredible demands on today's classroom teachers, no activity is worth doing unless it promises to make the central part of a teacher's work more successful and satisfying. Thus, selecting a focus, the first step in the process, is vitally important. Selecting a focus begins with the teacher researcher or the team of action researchers asking:

What element(s) of our practice or what aspect of student learning do we wish to investigate?

Step 2—Clarifying Theories

The second step involves identifying the values, beliefs, and theoretical perspectives the researchers hold relating to their focus. For example, if teachers are concerned about increasing responsible classroom behavior, it will be helpful for them to begin by clarifying which approach—using punishments and rewards, allowing students to experience the natural consequences of their behaviors, or some other strategy—they feel will work best in helping students acquire responsible classroom behavior habits.

Step 3—Identifying Research Questions

Once a focus area has been selected and the researcher's perspectives and beliefs about that focus have been clarified, the next step is to generate a set of personally meaningful research questions to guide the inquiry.

Step 4—Collecting Data

Professional educators always want their instructional decisions to be based on the best possible data. Action researchers can accomplish this by making sure that the data used to justify their actions are *valid* (meaning the information represents what the researchers say it does) and *reliable* (meaning the researchers are confident about the accuracy of their data). Lastly, before data are used to make teaching decisions, teachers must be confident that the lessons drawn from the data align with any unique characteristics of their classroom or school.

To ensure reasonable validity and reliability, action researchers should avoid relying on any single source of data. Most teacher researchers use a process called *triangulation* to enhance the validity and reliability of their findings. Basically, triangulation means using multiple independent sources of data to answer one's questions. Triangulation is like studying an object located inside a box by viewing it through various windows cut into the sides of the box. Observing a phenomenon through multiple "windows" can help a single researcher compare and contrast what is being seen through a variety of lenses.

When planning instruction, teachers want the techniques they choose to be appropriate for the unique qualities of their students. All teachers have had the experience of implementing a "research-proven" strategy only to have it fail with their students. The desire of teachers to use approaches that "fit" their particular students is not dissimilar to a doctor's concern that the specific medicine being prescribed be the correct one for the individual patient. The ability of the action research process to satisfy an educator's need for "fit" may be its most powerful attribute. Because the data being collected come from the very students and teachers who are engaged with the treatment, the relevance of the findings is assured.

For the harried and overworked teacher, "data collection" can appear to be the most intimidating aspect of the entire seven-step action research process. The question I am repeatedly asked, "Where will I find the time and expertise to develop valid and reliable instruments for data collection?", gives voice to a realistic fear regarding time management. Fortunately, classrooms and schools are, by their nature, data-rich environments. Each day a child is in class, he or she is producing or not producing work, is interacting productively with classmates or experiencing difficulties in social situations, and is completing assignments proficiently or poorly. Teachers not only see these events transpiring before their eyes, they generally record these events in their grade books. The key to managing triangulated data collection is, first, to be effective and efficient in collecting the material that is already swirling around the classroom, and, second, to identify other sources of data that might be effectively surfaced with tests, classroom discussions, or questionnaires.

Step 5—Analyzing Data

Although data analysis often brings to mind the use of complex statistical calculations, this is rarely the case for the action researcher. A number of relatively user-friendly procedures can help a practitioner identify the trends and patterns in action research data. During this portion of the seven-step process, teacher researchers will methodically sort, sift, rank, and examine their data to answer two generic questions:

- *What is the story told by these data?*
- *Why did the story play itself out this way?*

By answering these two questions, the teacher researcher can acquire a better understanding of the phenomenon under investigation and as a result can end up producing grounded theory regarding what might be done to improve the situation.

Step 6—Reporting Results

It is often said that teaching is a lonely endeavor. It is doubly sad that so many teachers are left alone in their classrooms to reinvent the wheel on a daily basis. The loneliness of teaching is unfortunate not only because of its inefficiency, but also because when dealing with complex problems the wisdom of several minds is inevitably better than one.

The sad history of teacher isolation may explain why the very act of reporting on their action research has proven so powerful for both the researchers and their colleagues. The reporting of action research most often occurs in informal settings that are far less intimidating than the venues where scholarly research has traditionally been shared. Faculty meetings, brown bag lunch seminars, and teacher conferences are among the most common venues for sharing action research with peers. However, each year more and more teacher researchers are writing up their work for publication or to help fulfill requirements in graduate programs. Regardless of which venue or technique educators select for reporting on research, the simple knowledge that they are making a contribution to a collective knowledge base regarding teaching and learning frequently proves to be among the most rewarding aspects of this work.

Step 7—Taking Informed Action

Taking informed action, or "action planning," the last step in the action research process, is very familiar to most teachers. When teachers write lesson plans or develop academic programs, they are engaged in the action planning process. What makes action planning particularly satisfying for the teacher researcher is that with each piece of data uncovered (about teaching or student learning) the educator will feel greater confidence in the wisdom of the next steps. Although all teaching can be classified as trial and error, action researchers find that the research process liberates them from continuously repeating their past mistakes. More important, with each refinement of practice, action researchers gain valid and reliable data on their developing virtuosity.

Three Purposes for Action Research

As stated earlier, action research can be engaged in by an individual teacher, a collaborative group of colleagues sharing a common concern, or an entire school faculty. These three different approaches to organizing for research serve three compatible, yet distinct, purposes:

- Building the reflective practitioner
- Making progress on schoolwide priorities
- Building professional cultures

Building the Reflective Practitioner

When individual teachers make a personal commitment to systematically collect data on their work, they are embarking on a process that will foster continuous growth and development. When each lesson is looked on as an empirical investigation into factors affecting teaching and learning and when reflections on the findings from each day's work inform the next day's instruction, teachers can't help but develop greater mastery of the art and science of teaching. In this way, the individual teachers conducting action research are making continuous progress in developing their strengths as reflective practitioners.

Making Progress on Schoolwide Priorities

Increasingly, schools are focusing on strengthening themselves and their programs through the development of common focuses and a strong sense of esprit de corps. Peters and Waterman (1982) in their landmark book, *In Search of Excellence,* called the achievement of focus "sticking to the knitting." When a faculty shares a commitment to achieving excellence with a specific focus—for example, the development of higher-order thinking, positive social behavior, or higher standardized test scores—then collaboratively studying their practice will not only contribute to the achievement of the shared goal but would have a powerful impact on team building and program development. Focusing the combined time, energy, and creativity of a group of committed professionals on a single pedagogical issue will inevitably lead to program improvements, as well as to the school becoming a "center of excellence." As a result, when a faculty chooses to focus on one issue and all the teachers elect to enthusiastically participate in action research on that issue, significant progress on the schoolwide priorities cannot help but occur.

Building Professional Cultures

Often an entire faculty will share a commitment to student development, yet the group finds itself unable to adopt a single common focus for action research. This should not be viewed as indicative of a problem. Just as the medical practitioners working at a "quality" medical center will hold a shared vision of a healthy adult, it is common for all the faculty members at a school to share a similar perspective on what constitutes a well-educated student. However, like the doctors at the medical center, the teachers in a "quality" school may well differ on which specific aspects of the shared vision they are most motivated to pursue at any point in time.

Schools whose faculties cannot agree on a single research focus can still use action research as a tool to help transform themselves into a learning organization. They accomplish this in the same manner as do the physicians at the medical center. It is common practice in a quality medical center for physicians to engage in independent, even idiosyncratic, research agendas. However, it is also common for medical researchers to share the findings obtained from their research with colleagues (even those engaged in other specialties).

School faculties who wish to transform themselves into "communities of learners" often empower teams of colleagues who share a passion about one aspect of teaching and learning to conduct investigations into that area of interest and then share what they've learned with the rest of the school community. This strategy allows an entire faculty to develop and practice the discipline that Peter Senge (1990) labeled "team learning." In these schools, multiple action research inquiries occur simultaneously, and no one is held captive to another's priority, yet everyone knows that all the work ultimately will be shared and will consequently contribute to organizational learning.

Why Action Research Now?

If ever there were a time and a strategy that were right for each other, the time is now and the strategy is action research! This is true for a host of reasons, with none more important than the need to accomplish the following:

- Professionalize teaching.
- Enhance the motivation and efficacy of a weary faculty.
- Meet the needs of an increasingly diverse student body.
- Achieve success with "standards-based" reforms.

Professionalizing Teaching

Teaching in North America has evolved in a manner that makes it more like blue-collar work than a professional undertaking. Although blue-collar workers are expected to do their jobs with vigilance and vigor, it is also assumed that their tasks will be routine, straightforward, and, therefore, easily handled by an isolated worker with only the occasional support of a supervisor.

Professional work, on the other hand, is expected to be complex and nonroutine, and will generally require collaboration among practitioners to produce satisfactory results. With the exploding knowledge base on teaching and learning and the heightened demands on teachers to help all children achieve mastery of meaningful objectives, the inadequacy of the blue-collar model for teaching is becoming much clearer.

When the teachers in a school begin conducting action research, their workplace begins to take on more of the flavor of the workplaces of other professionals. The wisdom that informs practice starts coming from those doing the work, not from supervisors who oftentimes are less in touch with and less sensitive to the issues of teaching and learning than the teachers doing the work. Furthermore, when teachers begin engaging their colleagues in discussions of classroom issues, the multiple perspectives that emerge and thus frame the dialogue tend to produce wiser professional decisions.

Enhancing Teacher Motivation and Efficacy

The work of teaching has always been difficult. But now it isn't just the demands of the classroom that are wearing teachers down. Students increasingly bring more problems into the classroom; parental and societal expectations keep increasing; and financial cutbacks make it clear that today's teachers are being asked to do more with less. Worse still, the respect that society had traditionally placed upon public school teachers is eroding, as teacher bashing and attacks on the very value of a public education are becoming a regular part of the political landscape. Consequently, teacher burnout has become the plague of the modern schoolhouse.

Many teachers now ask, "Am I making any difference?" Regardless of all the negative pressures on teachers, the sheer nobility of the work keeps many dedicated educators on the job, but only so long as they can get credible answers to the "efficacy" question. However, without credible evidence that the work of teaching is making a difference, it is hard to imagine the best and brightest sticking with such a difficult and poorly compensated line of work. Fortunately, evidence has shown that teachers who elect to integrate the use of data into their work start exhibiting the compulsive behavior of fitness enthusiasts who regularly weigh themselves, check their heart rate, and graph data on their improving physical development. For both teachers and athletes, the continuous presence of compelling data that their hard work is paying off becomes, in itself, a vitally energizing force.

Meeting the Needs of a Diverse Student Body

In a homogeneous society in which all students come to school looking alike, it might be wise to seek the one right answer to questions of pedagogy. But, as anyone who has recently visited an American classroom can attest, it is rare to find any two children for whom the same intervention could ever be "right on target." The days are gone when it was possible to believe that all a teacher had to do was master and deliver the grade-level curriculum. It is now imperative that classroom teachers have strong content background in each of the subjects they teach, be familiar with the range of student differences in their classrooms, and be capable of diagnosing and prescribing appropriate instructional modifications based upon a knowledge of each child's uniqueness.

Crafting solutions to these dynamic and ever changing classroom issues can be an exciting undertaking, especially when one acknowledges that newer and better answers are evolving all the time. Nevertheless, great personal satisfaction comes from playing a role in creating successful solutions to continually changing puzzles. Conversely, if teachers are expected to robotically implement outdated approaches, especially when countless new challenges are arriving at their door, the frustration can become unbearable.

Achieving Success in a Standards-Based System

In most jurisdictions standards-driven accountability systems have become the norm. Although they differ somewhat from state to state and province to province, fundamentally these standards-based systems have certain things in common. Specifically, most education departments and ministries have declared that they expect the standards to be rigorous and meaningful, and that they expect all students to meet the standards at the mastery level.

The stakes in the standards movement are high. Students face consequences regarding promotion and graduation. Teachers and schools face ridicule and loss of funding if they fail to meet community expectations. Of course, none of that would be problematic if we as a society knew with certainty how to achieve universal student success. However, the reality is that no large system anywhere in the world has ever been successful in getting *every* student to master a set of meaningful objectives. If we accept the truth of that statement, then we need to acknowledge the fact that achieving the goal of universal student mastery will not be easy. That said, most people will agree it is a most noble endeavor in which to invest energy and a worthy goal for any faculty to pursue.

The reality is that our public schools will not prevail with the challenges inherent in the standards movement unless they encourage experimentation, inquiry, and dialogue by those pioneers (the teachers) who are working toward meeting those challenges. For this reason, it is imperative that these 21st century pioneers, our classroom teachers, conduct the research on "standards attainment" themselves.

So the time is right for action research. The teachers, schools, and school systems that seize this opportunity and begin investing in the power of inquiry will find that they are re-creating the professional practice of education in their locale as a meaningful and rewarding pursuit. Conversely, school systems that enter the 21st century unwilling to invest in the "wisdom of practice" will likely find it increasingly hard to fill their classrooms with enough teachers who are both capable of and willing to tackle the challenges that lie ahead.

2 How Is Action Research Accomplished?

Chapter 1 identified and defined the seven steps of the action research process. This chapter identifies some specific activities that teachers can engage in as they work their way through this process. To illustrate some possible activities, I will now walk through the seven steps and discuss how I might have addressed them when teaching writing to 9th grade students.

Step 1—Finding a Focus

The first step of the action research process calls for a significant investment of time and energy. Because of the time pressure experienced by classroom teachers, the annual ritual of choosing professional development goals and school improvement targets usually doesn't receive the reflective time that it deserves. This becomes costly in at least two ways. Often teachers end up committing themselves to work on projects that, upon later consideration, weren't really worth their time. And, on other occasions, although the educational outcomes teachers pursued might have been worthwhile, the interventions that were hurriedly adopted often turn out to be an inadequate match for the local situation. Both of these problems can be avoided if teachers are encouraged and supported in becoming more deliberate in their planning.

So how can busy teachers work through the "getting ready" process while at the same time attending to those other issues vying for their limited time? The following strategies have proved helpful for many teacher researchers who are searching for a meaningful focus.

Strategy 1—The Reflective Journal

A good way to find a focus is to use a reflective journal. This process begins by creating a prompt that will provide a focus for daily reflections for a limited number of days. For example, I might elect to spend 10 minutes a day for two weeks responding to the following prompt: What occurred today in my writing class that went well, poorly, or was a surprise to me? Why do I think these occurrences are significant?

After writing 10 daily responses to this prompt, I can stop, reread my work, and see which issues were repeated and what trends emerged, if any. For example, I might find myself repeatedly fretting over the lack of attention my students were giving to the editing process. Such journal entries could help me identify the following two concerns: (1) my students behave as though my expectations were for them to simply fill up a page with words; (2) my students appear willing to accept significant sloppiness with mechanics, word choice, and syntax in their final papers. Furthermore, my journal observations could help me see that my constant nagging about the importance of revision was going unheard, or at least unheeded, by a number of my students.

In this case, the use of the journal could have helped me understand that "learning how to be more effective in the encouragement of editing" was a focus that would benefit both me and my students.

Strategy 2—The Reflective Interview

The reflective interview is a focusing technique that is valuable when colleagues are interested in working as a group; however, an individual teacher can also use this process when developing a focus for a solo inquiry. Whether being used for a one-person project or for group work, the reflective interview requires the assistance of a colleague.

The reflective interview is a verbal process that produces insights similar to those produced through journaling. However, with the reflective interview, teachers talk through their concerns rather than write about them. The rules for the reflective interview are few and simple:

• Find a location where you are unlikely to be interrupted for at least 30 minutes.
• Select a colleague who is willing to listen as you talk.
• Pick a topic to talk about that meets the following criteria: (1) it concerns teaching or learning; (2) it is an issue of significant personal concern; (3) improving performance on this issue is within your control.

• Explain to your colleague that his or her job is to listen, ask clarifying questions if necessary, and stimulate further reflection (should you run out of things to say in less than 30 minutes).

When engaged in a reflective interview on my problem, implementing the writing process, I likely would speak of my concerns regarding the quality of the finished work the students were turning in. I might also express my frustration over seeing students repeat the same errors in each piece of their written work and their apparent willingness to accept as complete products that were far from finished. As the interview progressed, I might even share my concern that the approach I had been using, nagging, wasn't producing the desired results. Not only was it not assisting my students with their writing, but, I might observe, it was having a detrimental impact on classroom climate. I can almost hear myself telling my colleague, "I've become so frustrated with this group of kids that I'm not even sure I want to teach language arts anymore!"

Here my colleague might join in, perhaps with questions like these: "Has this always been a problem for you or just with this particular group of students?" "Are you aware of any other strategies that teachers have used successfully?"

Generally it takes only a question or two to get my thoughts flowing again. Following such a query I might state that I've heard a number of teachers speak glowingly about the use of "peer editing." However, I might also share my fear that with this current group of students, offering any opportunity for peer work would be an invitation to get further off task, and so on.

After 30 minutes of listening, it is time for the colleague to paraphrase what he or she heard. Often just hearing ideas reported back through another person's voice is enough to help surface patterns in one's concerns and, consequently, insights into what is worth taking the time to research. In this case I would likely conclude that an excellent focus for my research might be finding ways to productively motivate and assist my students with the revision of their written work.

Strategy 3—Analytic Discourse

This process, somewhat similar to the reflective interview, is most often used by a group of colleagues intending to pursue a research study collaboratively. In such cases one member of the group, someone acknowledged to have thought quite a bit about the issue, becomes the subject for a group interview. The interviewers are then expected to probe and push the interviewee in order to cause that person to reflect deeply on the topic at hand. The purpose of the analytic discourse is to get the individual being interviewed to explore the topic as fully as possible. As with the reflective interview, the following rules must be followed to maximize the success of the analytic discourse:

- Interviewers ask probing questions.
- Interviewers offer no personal opinions.
- No critical comments are permitted.

Generally, the analytic discourse surfaces and addresses most major issues surrounding a topic after 30 to 40 minutes. However, the discourse should not be considered complete until the interviewee feels that he or she has no more to say on the topic.

Step 2—Clarifying Theories

Whatever strategy is used to surface an area of concern, the next step involves making explicit one's underlying feelings, beliefs, and insights regarding the problem or focus. It is helpful early in the action research process to explore theoretical perspectives or biases that an individual researcher or members of a research group may hold regarding the research focus. The two strategies suggested below—the priority pie and the graphic reconstruction—have proven effective for both individual and group inquiries.

The Priority Pie

The priority pie is a mechanism that helps teacher researchers identify those variables that they perceive as being most relevant to their issue. It also helps clarify personal beliefs about the relative importance of those variables. The priority pie process has three steps: (1) brainstorming, (2) conducting an intuitive assessment, and (3) drawing a pictorial representation.

First, the researcher individually brainstorms a list in response to the question:

What are the most significant factors or variables that will need to be addressed if I am to be successful helping students address this issue?

If I were making a priority pie regarding my issue with student editing, I might list the following factors or variables:

- Knowledge of grammatical rules

- Ability to choose and use a variety of voices
- Working vocabulary
- Motivation regarding quality work
- Comfort with criticism
- Word processing skills

After brainstorming a list of factors, the researcher needs to make a judgment about the relative influence of the listed variables by assigning a percent to each item (corresponding to that item's importance to achieving the whole). The sum of the individual percentages must equal 100 percent. In my case, I might assign these percentages:

• Knowledge of grammatical rules	25%
• Use of a variety of voices	5%
• Vocabulary	15%
• Motivation	25%
• Comfort with criticism	15%
• Word processing skills	15%
TOTAL	100%

Finally, the researcher displays the assigned percentages on a pie chart. The resulting pie graph becomes a rough visual portrayal of the initial theory held by the researcher. In my case, the priority pie (Figure 2.1) would alert me to the relative value of the variables that I believe need to be attended to if I am to succeed with my goal.

Graphic Reconstruction

The graphic reconstruction is a process used to further develop and explore a researcher's theoretical perspective on the issue to be investigated. In addition, it will elaborate on the researcher's ideas on how performance might be improved in this area. The product that results form this process looks like a mind map or the kind of "web" teachers often have students produce as a prewriting exercise. The function of the graphic reconstruction is to fully illustrate the researcher's understanding of the dynamic relationships between the variables identified in the priority pie. A graphic reconstruction of my perspective on how the editing process should work with my writing class would look like Figure 2.2.

At this point, it is appropriate to investigate what others have found out about the same topic. It is prudent for a researcher or an action research team to review computer databases (such as ERIC) and text

FIGURE 2.1

Priority Pie—The Development of Editing Proficiency

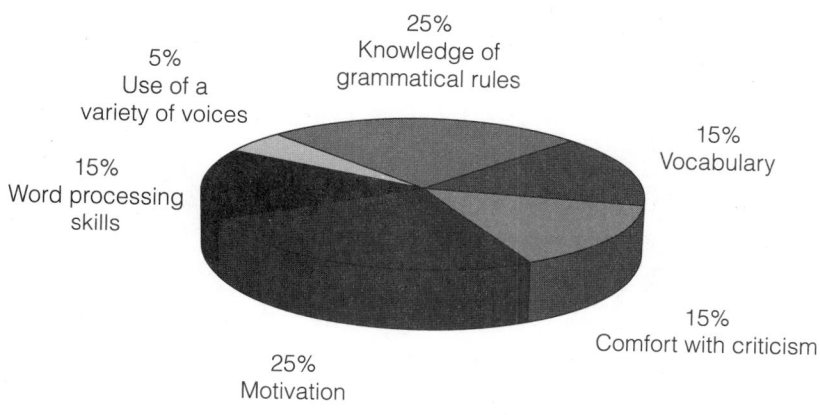

resources to identify other perspectives on the issue that are worth considering before initiating action. This step can help avoid getting too far down the road pursuing ideas that others have already thoroughly investigated.

After completing a literature review, it is time to return to the graphic reconstruction to determine whether changes to this illustration of your theoretical perspective are now necessary based upon the data, findings, and insights of other investigators.

Step 3—Identifying Research Questions

The next step involves reflecting on one's focus and theory in order to identify a question or a set of questions that merit an investment of time and energy. This is accomplished by returning to the graphic reconstruction to reflect on the following key question:

What significant aspect(s) of my theory am I relatively uncertain about and, therefore, wish or need to know more about?

FIGURE 2.2
A Graphic Reconstruction—The Development of Student Editors

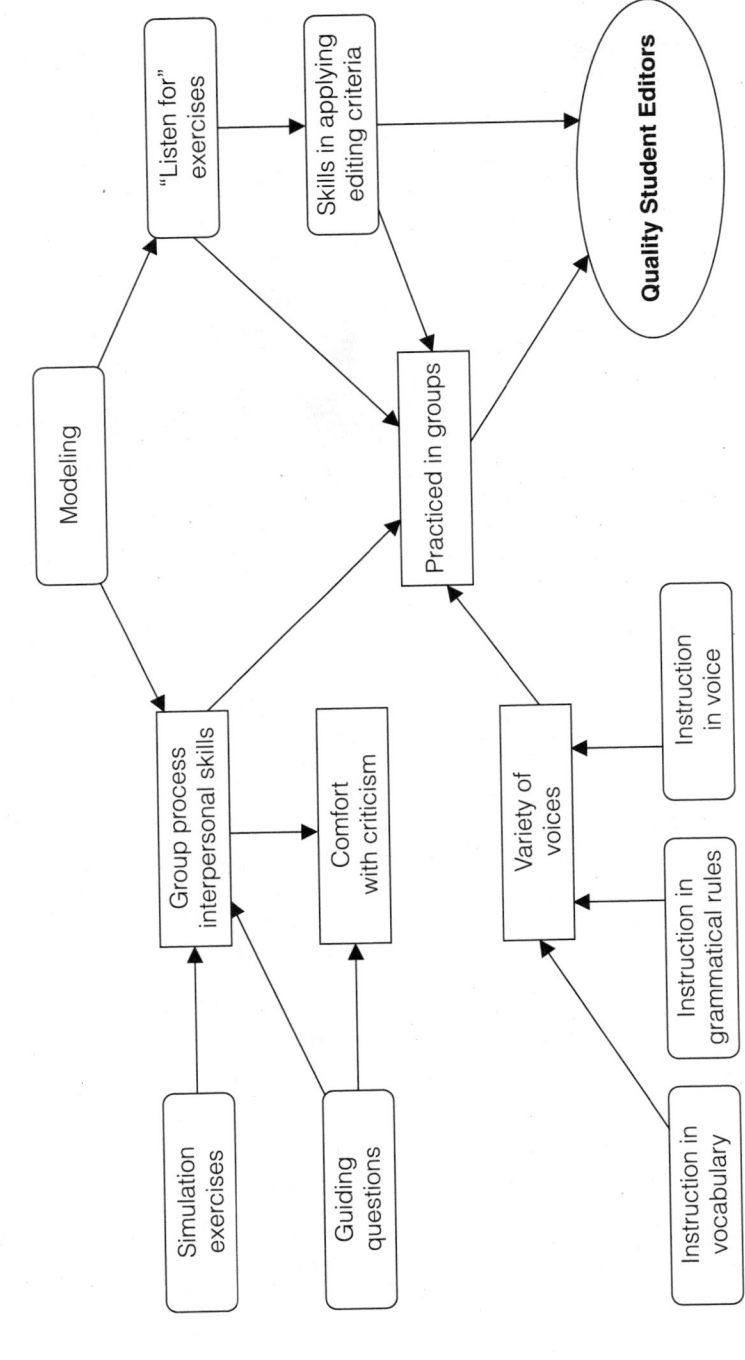

In the case of my inquiry regarding the improvement of student editing, several possible research questions might emerge. For example, What is the relationship between student enjoyment of writing and the quality of their editing? In what ways will providing students an advance copy of a scoring rubric have an effect on the quality of their finished papers? To what extent are finished papers different when peer editing is employed?

Step 4—Data Collection

When collecting and analyzing data, action researchers can do a great deal to ensure the validity and reliability of their findings by using a process called triangulation. The term *triangulation* refers to the use of multiple independent data sources to corroborate findings. The purpose and necessity of corroboration is the same for the action researcher as it is for the trial lawyer. A trial lawyer knows that to convince a jury of the accuracy of a legal theory, it helps to have more than one witness; the more individual witnesses whose testimony supports the theory, the more credible the theory becomes.

Educational action researchers usually have a wide variety of data sources available to them. Some of the most common sources are the following:

Existing data
- School/teacher records
- Student work/portfolios

Observation data
- Photographs
- Videotapes
- Diaries, logs, journals
- Rating scales/rubrics
- Data obtained by shadowing students through the school day

Probes
- Tests
- Surveys
- Interviews
- Focus groups

A helpful tool for planning data collection and triangulation is a *triangulation matrix*—a simple grid that shows the various data sources that will be used to answer each research question. The matrix provides the action researcher with some assurance that the potential for bias (which is always present whenever a single source of data is used) won't take on undue significance. Figure 2.3 illustrates how a completed triangulation matrix for my study on student editing might look.

Step 5—Data Analysis

During Step 5, data analysis, the teacher researcher engages in a systematic effort to search for patterns or trends in the data. There are many ways to accomplish this. Regardless of the particular technique employed, during the analysis phase the researcher tries to systematically cut, sift, and sort the data into piles of like or similar objects. The key purpose of this systematic sorting and categorizing is to assist in answering the following two questions:

> *What is the story told by my data?*
> *What might explain this story?*

Once the researcher believes the process has resulted in adequate answers to those two questions, it is time for one final return to the graphic reconstruction. This time the researcher takes a critical look at the initial theory and asks how it may need to be revised based upon the analysis of the data.

Steps 6 and 7—Reporting and Action Planning

The primary purpose of action research is to inform the decision making of practitioners who wish to improve their performance. This was the case in the example of my work on student editing. For this reason, when an individual teacher is doing the action research on an individual problem, it is less necessary to make the last two steps of the process—reporting and action planning—public or formal. In my case, it might have been enough for me to simply see what worked and in which circumstances and then to adjust my instructional planning accordingly. If the teacher researcher wishes to share his or her findings, popular venues include grade-level or departmental meetings, faculty forums, or parent-teacher meetings. The choice of reporting venue ultimately resides with the researcher, but the purpose for the sharing should always be the same: to invite open and collegial dialogue on ways educators can enhance student learning.

FIGURE 2.3

Triangulation Matrix—Study on Student Editing

Research Question	Data Source #1	Data Source #2	Data Source #3
What is the relationship between student enjoyment of writing and the quality of their editing?	Student survey	Analysis of first, second, and final drafts	Comparison with work on previous assignments
In what ways will providing students with a copy of a scoring rubric impact the quality of their finished papers?	Student interviews	Contrast between revisions made in assignments without rubrics and ones with rubrics	Third-party assessments of finished products
To what extent are the finished papers different when students use peer editors?	Student interviews	Contrast between revisions made in assignments without peer editing and ones completed with peer editing	Third-party assessments of finished products

When, however, the rationale for engaging in the research is school improvement (as opposed to teacher development), then a public, inclusive, and participatory process for reporting and the subsequent action planning is absolutely necessary. The final section of this book (Part IV) provides specific guidance on ways to use action research as part of a collaborative, culture-building process to advance a school improvement agenda.

A Shift in Focus

Chapters 1 and 2 introduced the process of action research and described some of the ways it has been carried out in schools. I hope this discussion has intrigued you enough to encourage you to learn more about specific practices engaged in by practitioner researchers.

However, these days it takes more than an intriguing idea to get an educator's full attention. Never before have teachers faced so many demands. Not only are the complexity and diversity of today's students and the issues they bring into classrooms more challenging than ever, but the expectations that society holds for academic performance have never been higher. Teachers who are already working as hard as they can must attend to new state standards, high-stakes testing programs, graduation requirements, and college admissions standards. In most locales teachers are being asked to incorporate new technologies, new evaluation procedures, and alternative teaching methods into their daily routines. Furthermore, all of this is happening during a period of declining resources and increased class sizes. Having a good idea to share (like action research) is not enough to garner the full attention of today's educator.

For this reason, I'd like to pause for a moment, step back from this examination of research methods, and shift attention to why I believe the present time, even with all of its pressures, is a most propitious time for implementing the strategies and techniques of reflective practice. The next two chapters discuss the context of public education in North America at the turn of the 21st century and present a rationale for investing time in action research.

I believe we are at a crossroads. The particular actions and decisions that educators make in the first years of the 21st century will likely determine the future and nature of the education profession. The pressures currently being exerted on classroom teachers could result in a return to highly bureaucratic structures in schools or, alternatively, give rise to a radical restructuring of the role of the classroom teacher. In the following two chapters I present the case that if we truly wish this era of reform to result in a renewal of the inherent nobility of teaching, then this is "prime time" to invest in teacher research.

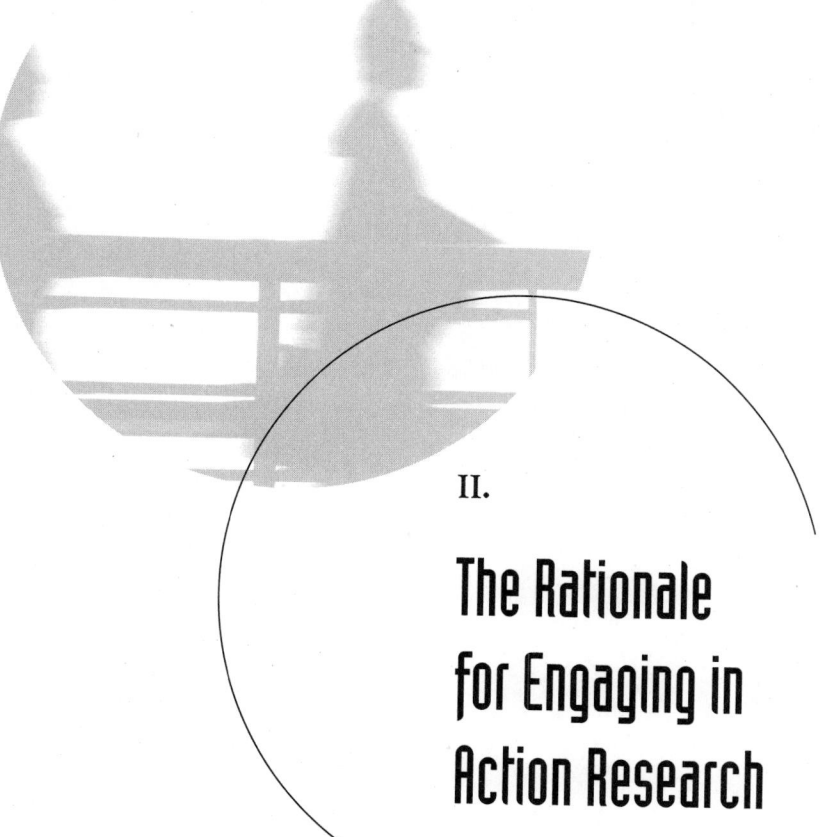

II.

The Rationale
for Engaging in
Action Research

3 Professionalism, Teacher Efficacy, and Standards-Based Education

Consider how it would feel to be a participant in either of the following two scenarios.

Scenario 1: A group of classroom teachers has gathered for the first faculty meeting of the year. The superintendent of schools, with a pained look on his face, convenes the meeting by saying:

> I'm sure you are all aware of the governor's new educational reform plan. The new state standards have purposefully been set high, and our students have a long history of scoring well below state averages on similar standardized tests. But now the stakes have been raised! Beginning this spring, each school's scores on the state proficiency test will be published over the Internet. Worse, the date for reporting on our scores has been set just two weeks before our annual levy election. According to the statute, if more than 50 percent of our kids fail to meet standards in reading, math, writing, or science, our district will be placed on probation and will become subject to state takeover. Understand, therefore, that I'm not kidding when I say that improving academic performance needs to be the number-one priority for each and every one of you!

Scenario 2: Now imagine a group of engineers at a large aerospace company who have just been called to a meeting facilitated by the corporate CEO. With a broad smile on her face, she approaches the podium saying:

> Welcome to the future! As I suspect you have all read in the company newsletter, NASA has offered us the opportunity to develop a viable plan for a manned mission to Mars to be completed in the next 10 years. This mission will present us with numerous obstacles, many of which are far greater than any we have successfully faced in the past. Succeeding with this mission will require achieving breakthroughs in computer technology, in our energy systems, in our life support systems, and in the design of the spacecraft itself. To add to this challenge, NASA is unlikely to provide a budget anywhere as large as that which was available for the Apollo and space shuttle programs. I'm sure you share my view that this is a most exciting project; one that will take all the creativity and energy we can muster if we expect to prevail. So let's get at it!

Chances are the teachers leaving the faculty meeting depicted in the first scenario would be deflated and frustrated. The superintendent's message would have overwhelmed all the excitement they had felt earlier about starting the year with a new group of kids. In all likelihood, many of the teachers interpreted the speech this way:

Our boss thinks—
• It's our fault that the students haven't been doing better.
• The primary reason for the district's history of poor performance is that we haven't been working hard enough and improving academic performance hasn't been our priority.
• If this situation doesn't change, we will be subjected to public embarrassment or worse.
• We are expected to already know all that we need to know in order to improve.

The corporate CEO's message to the aerospace engineers would likely have been interpreted very differently. The engineers probably walked away from the meeting feeling personally and intellectually challenged. They probably understood the CEO as saying something like this:

• I'm asking you to accomplish something very difficult.
• The challenges ahead are far tougher than those faced by earlier generations of aerospace engineers.

• Ultimately our success will depend upon our collective problem-solving skills and creativity.

If you were among those engineers, you would likely feel inspired as well as humbled by the realization that you were standing at the very outer limits of scientific know-how. Although you might feel anxious about the challenges ahead and realize that overcoming these challenges would require great energy and creativity, you would, no doubt, be excited about the mission and eager to get going. Acknowledging the possibility of failures and setbacks along the way would neither discourage nor deter you from accepting the challenge.

It is unfortunate that the tone of those two scenarios is so different, because in many ways the challenge placed before a "rocket scientist" is quite similar to the challenge faced by today's classroom teachers. Not infrequently, when someone appears confused about a simple endeavor, someone else says sarcastically, "Hey, this isn't rocket science!" That has become a crude shorthand way of saying that the task at hand isn't all that complex. I would argue that being a classroom teacher at the start of the 21st century is every bit as complex as "rocket science." In truth, upon close examination and relative to public school teaching, rocket science ought to be considered pretty simple stuff!

Consider that today's typical classroom is far more diverse and complex than ever before. Learning disabled students sit next to gifted students. Students with behavioral disorders and children who began life as "crack babies" join in cooperative learning groups with students whose parents don't speak a word of English. The child of an aggressive corporate CEO may be engaged in a discussion with a child of poverty. Not only do today's classrooms contain students with a wider variety of developmental experiences than ever before, but society's expectations for student performance (as evidenced by the proliferation of standards legislation) have never been higher. Add to this mixture the fact that no one appears willing to tolerate even the slightest setback or failure as educators and schools work feverishly on restructuring.

The scenario that began this chapter isn't far-fetched. Virtually every state and province in North America now expects (through regulation and legislation) their public schools to prepare students to prevail with a high-caliber curriculum. Furthermore, they are demanding more than seat time as a measure; they want the reassurance that comes from quality assessments. These expectations can be clearly seen in legislation that demands that students demonstrate mastery or proficiency on tough new standards.

No doubt about it, the standards movement presents an incredible challenge for today's educator. Assisting every public school student to achieve mastery with meaningful standards is an enormous undertaking. Anyone who doubts that assertion should consider that, throughout the world, no school system, no country, no state, no city has ever been successful in making every child an academic success. For centuries, that easily stated but hard to achieve goal has eluded the world's best educators, much as interplanetary travel has eluded "rocket scientists."

The question that all this raises for me is, why would being asked to accomplish the "impossible" be motivating and exciting if we were "rocket scientists," yet frustrating to us as educators? I believe the answer lies in both the way the challenge has been posed and the way that the pioneers are being asked to accomplish their missions. I'll elaborate.

The easiest part of any endeavor is the issuing of the challenge, whether it comes from the president of the United States pledging to send a man to the moon by the end of the decade or a state legislature asserting that every child will demonstrate mastery of a rigorous curriculum by the end of high school. However, as the aerospace engineer in the example above might contend, the really exciting part comes later, when they are engaged in the experimentation that will be necessary to find the answers to those questions that once seemed so impossible to answer.

The challenges immediately ahead for public school educators are no less significant than those once asked of the scientists working on the Apollo mission. As noted earlier, never in humankind's history has any school system figured out how to enable every student to meet high standards on meaningful objectives. Is that goal potentially achievable? I think it is. Yet, unless we truly believe there has been a conspiracy to deny good educational practice to the world's children, we need to acknowledge that numerous breakthroughs, no less substantial than those that were needed to get Neil Armstrong and Buzz Aldrin to the moon, will be required on the road to universal scholastic excellence.

In Chapter 1, I stated that in many places educators are treated more like blue-collar workers than true professionals, and "reprofessionalizing teaching" was one important reason to engage in action research. This is an important issue that deserves further discussion.

Reprofessionalizing Teaching

In the scenarios that opened this chapter, the teachers and the engineers were addressed in a very different fashion. The engineers were challenged as a group of professionals, individuals assumed to have the capacity to think their way through complex undertakings. The teachers, on the other hand, were addressed as workers, individuals who needed to be admonished to buckle down and work harder.

Although there is no single simple explanation for this distinction, the structure of teachers' work and the expectations that school systems place on teachers are major contributors to this state of affairs. In Chapter 1 and elsewhere (Sagor, 1993), I've discussed the consequences of organizing teaching in a blue-collar manner rather than as a professional endeavor. Simply put, blue-collar workers are expected to faithfully implement the directives of more "capable" and more highly trained supervisors. In jobs such as repetitive assembly line work, it is assumed that workers will perform their tasks best when isolated from distractions and other workers, and furthermore, it is widely assumed that the workers won't need a great deal of training because the tasks are rather straightforward. Basically, the assumption is that blue-collar workers' contributions to the enterprise can be measured by the extent of their loyalty and the sweat of their brows. With nonprofessional work, it is assumed that the qualities of creativity, initiative, and entrepreneurship will be supplied by the "bosses," not the workers.

Our expectations of professionals are quite different. These people are expected to have the ability to attack nonroutine problems and to do so creatively. Therefore, they are expected to collaborate with others, to employ a variety of viewpoints, and ultimately to produce the very knowledge and insight that move their profession forward. Consequently, when the outcome obtained from a hardworking professional falls short of expectations, it is most often attributed to failings inherent in the intervention or treatment attempted, not on the merit or "worthiness" of the practitioner. In contrast, when a blue-collar worker fails to meet expectations, it is more likely blamed on worker incompetence.

Is it any wonder then that professionals tend to feel challenged when given a difficult task to perform? In fact, it is easy to understand why professionals get excited about being asked to push the "edge of the envelope." It also is easy to understand why many blue-collar workers logically conclude that their interests are best served by "dropping out" emotionally or simply employing the safest and most risk-free strategy.

Workers in bureaucratic enterprises often find it more important to get the boss off their back than to produce a quality product.

The tendency to organize teaching as if it were a blue-collar enterprise helps explain why many teachers react to the standards movement and other challenges by dropping out emotionally or becoming part of the epidemic of teacher burnout. Throughout North America, teacher bashing has become a predictable political ritual. The fact that our schools aren't more effective is blamed on "lazy teachers" or their unions. Some people argue that if society were only free from these "self-serving public employees," and we either educated our students at home or in private schools, academic achievement would immediately soar. How long does a person need to hear the blaming and name calling before frustration and giving up take over?

Occasionally the blame isn't placed upon the teachers directly. The methods and interventions used in schools also receive their share of criticism. It may be the "new" approach to the teaching of language, math, or science, or a new strategy for integrating curriculum that receives the blame. But right below the surface of that criticism is a belief that the folks to blame are those "flaky" educators who are implementing those "bad" strategies. This isn't totally illogical. Blaming teachers for the strategies they use would be fair if the teachers played a significant role in creating curriculum or designing instructional strategies. But it is rarely the teachers who write the textbooks; they aren't the ones teaching the graduate courses; they aren't the lobbyists selling the restructuring plan to the legislature. No, it isn't the teaching profession that drives educational innovation, research, and policy; but it is teachers who end up shouldering most of the blame.

Over the past decade industry has begun to learn important lessons. Deming (1986) and others in the Total Quality Management movement have helped enlightened businesses to understand that when workers face complex problems and are denied appropriate discretion on how to complete their work, it is only logical to expect them to retreat into an excuse-making mode. This explains why, in traditional organizations, frustrated workers may argue with their managers and ask questions like these: How can you expect success when we work with these inadequate tools? How can you expect us to build a quality product if you give us such miserable raw material?

Understanding the perspective of the alienated worker makes it easier to understand why classroom teachers express sentiments like these: How do they expect us to succeed with kids from this neighborhood and

from these families? With class sizes this large and saddled with an out-
moded curriculum, it would take a miracle for any of these kids to learn!

When we hear workers trying to escape personal responsibility by
blaming conditions outside of their control, their words provide testimony to a lack of confidence that they can prevail. Psychologists refer to
this as an expression of "low efficacy." The importance of believing in
one's ability to prevail even when pitted against great obstacles is a phenomenon most of us appreciate. It's the theme of a story that parents and
primary school teachers are very familiar with—*The Little Engine That
Could.* The cliché "If you think you can, you can, but if you think you
can't, you can't" underscores one of the most critical issues facing today's
educator—personal and collective efficacy.

Had the engineers who worked at NASA not believed that they
would prevail in getting a man to the moon, they would never have accomplished all that was required to realize that goal. Likewise, the success of legislatively mandated reforms will ultimately come down to
whether or not the "engineers" in charge (the teachers) are given credible reasons to believe that they can and will prevail.

As it stands now, the sad reality is that far too many teachers, faculties, and school systems lack the belief that they can make the breakthroughs necessary to achieve universal and fundamental student
success. Unless or until teachers sincerely believe that these accomplishments are within their power, all these glorious legislative reforms will
be doomed to failure.

Action Research as a Professional Pursuit

Even those who agree with my contention about the efficacy and morale
of today's educators might still ask why I feel that systematically engaging in teacher research will improve the situation. To answer this, it is
worth examining again the key differences between professional and
blue-collar work as discussed above:

- Professionals are expected to attack nonroutine problems and to
do so creatively.
- Professionals are expected to consider a variety of perspectives
when making decisions.
- Professionals play a significant role in producing the knowledge
and insights that move their profession forward.
- Professionals hold themselves accountable for using best practices.

Attacking Nonroutine Problems

When "told" to implement an "adopted" strategy and do it precisely as the instructor's manual suggests, the implication is that all students and classrooms are alike, and, therefore, one approach will prove appropriate for all situations. But teachers know by experience that this simply isn't the case. Nothing in teaching is ever routine. Just because a strategy worked second period doesn't mean it will succeed with the fifth-period class. However, when teachers have conducted action research on what has worked in their classrooms with a unique mix of students, they have uncovered ways to creatively handle nonroutine problems.

Considering Multiple Perspectives

When teachers are expected to work as loners, isolated in their own classrooms, they are being told that no more than one perspective is ever needed to make sound instructional decisions on behalf of a child. However, when teachers are encouraged to share their data on student performance and the findings of their action research, and to use these findings to construct alternative approaches for working with individual children or unique classes, they will see how multiple perspectives inevitably lead to better professional decisions.

Building a Professional Knowledge Base

It is understandable why many teachers are skeptical of educational research. Too frequently, the very voice of the researcher gives rise to practitioner suspicion. Teachers are wary of findings from people who they suspect have never been in the classroom, or who have little or no experience with the types of students who are attending their school. However, when teachers recognize their own perspective in the words and findings of researchers, when educational research truly reflects an understanding of the dynamics of today's classroom, teachers will not only find discussions around data to be relevant, but they will become eager to join in the debate with their own findings and insights.

Accountability

Most school accountability systems are predicated on assessments provided by outsiders or people occupying a higher rung on the bureaucratic ladder. The state holds school districts accountable, and principals and other supervisors assess and evaluate the quality of the teaching in their school. That isn't the norm in professional practice. My lawyer doesn't provide me with good service because she is afraid of getting a poor evaluation, nor does my physician treat me well because of fear of a reprimand from the hospital administrator. When teachers have timely data on performance and feel empowered to make appropriate changes based upon those data, then they will begin to feel greater efficacy and a greater willingness to hold themselves to the highest standards of professional performance.

In short, teachers in conventional settings often have feelings of low efficacy and lack a professional self-image. However, research has shown that teachers who regularly engage in collaborative practices, such as action research, develop high efficacy, a professional ethos, and their schools are marked by stronger faculty morale—most important, their students begin to perform better than before. Figure 3.1 is a graphic representation of my theoretical perspective on how action research relates to the school improvement process.

Using Data to Build Efficacy

Activating the power of reflective practice requires two things: (1) making data on performance available and (2) providing teachers the authority to use these data for the improvement of their instruction.

By now it should be clear why the superintendent's speech presented at the start of this chapter was futile. Telling hard-working educators (or students, for that matter) to simply work harder (as though that is all that is required for success) is not the answer. Schools don't need teachers to do *more* work; rather, schools should be encouraging teachers to do *different* work. School improvement and teacher efficacy are two concepts that are inextricably intertwined. Reasonable people do not change present practice unless or until they have credible data that causes them to believe improvement will result. This is an example of the behavioral phenomenon called "cognitive dissonance"; changes in behavior are unlikely to occur without changes in attitudes and beliefs.

If what schools need from teachers is not more work but better work, where should educators go to gain the insights and learn new skills? How can schools build greater institutional capacity?

Over the past half-century, most states and local districts have focused their hopes and investments on program implementation. Policymakers apparently believe that the secret to student success is finding and adopting the "right approach." Once the adoption is complete, all that is required is finding ways to motivate the teachers to get on with

FIGURE 3.1

Action Research and School Improvement

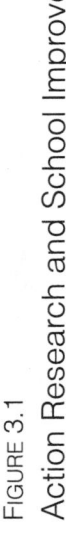

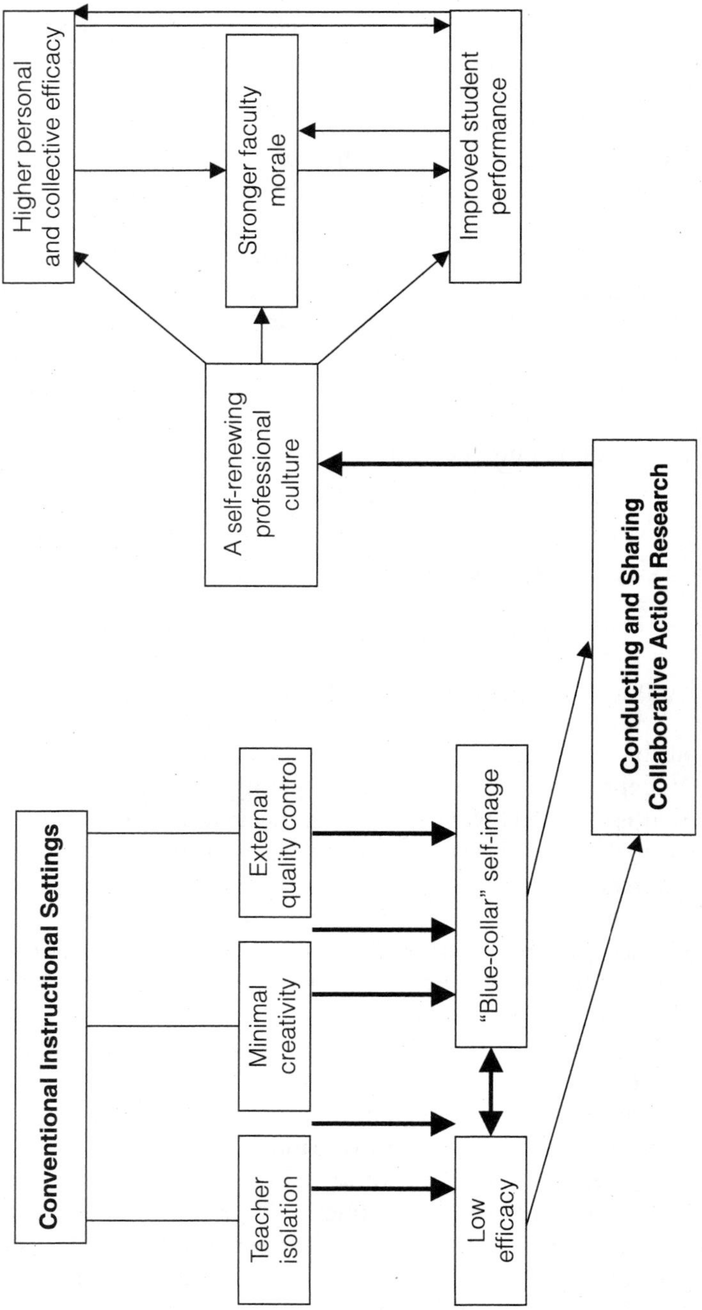

the implementation. It shouldn't surprise anyone that this approach hasn't worked any better than it has. Programs can only do so much for so many. Just as medical researchers will never find one antibiotic that will cure all infections, educators are unlikely to find a single reading program that succeeds with all learners. The search for the "teacher-proof" solution is and always will be a futile one. Therefore, if significant improvement over past waves of reform is the goal, it is time to cool our infatuation with programs and instead escalate our investments in people. This is why integrating action research into school life is so imperative.

Whatever else action research may be, it clearly is a statement of faith in the innate capacity of working educators. When schools provide support for teacher researchers by making data available and being open to the findings of classroom inquiry, they are investing in the development of their most valuable resource—their people. What teachers learn from and about their practice never fades. Each day educators can build upon the lessons learned from the day before. When teachers are encouraged to share their learning, the collective capacity of the school grows geometrically.

The two critical factors mentioned earlier—availability of data on performance and teacher authority to use the data to improve their instruction—are the prerequisites for building efficacy. As another example, individual student athletes can do extraordinary things when they have information and the power to use it. And in the Apollo mission, the team of professionals who were empowered to combine their creativity with available data and to devise the necessary technologies were able to accomplish the "impossible." This is the power of action research. It is a means to renew the efficacy that most teachers possessed when they left college, believing they could accomplish miracles.

4 Teaching: A Complex Process

Chapter 3 identified two key reasons to make action research a part of our school improvement work:

- The need to make teaching a more "professional" pursuit
- The motivational power of data for building teacher efficacy

This chapter examines two current trends that make investing in teacher research imperative:

- The increased diversity of our student bodies
- The high-stakes consequences of the standards movement

For people who don't enjoy a challenge, choosing to become a teacher is the worst possible career decision. Nothing in the schoolhouse works easily or smoothly. In fact, few if any schools can claim to perform as consistently as NASA's space shuttle. This isn't because the space shuttle is a simple machine—which it isn't—but because success in education, like all other human endeavors, is influenced by an infinite array of variables.

Although building a space shuttle is not a simple matter, the variables that an engineer needs to consider are determinable, manageable, and (generally) stable. Contrast the work of the engineer with that of the classroom teacher. Are the issues she faces manageable, determinable, and stable? To answer that question, let's look at a routine task encountered daily by a primary school classroom teacher: lesson planning for a diverse classroom.

A layperson might ask, "Just how hard could it be to design a math lesson for 7-year-olds?" Even when an instructional task seems straightforward, a teacher must consider many things. Imagine that the lesson being planned is a simple one—the addition of two-digit numbers with regrouping. What data does a typical 2nd grade teacher need to consider to properly design this lesson? Certainly if this lesson is to work for a particular child, the teacher should take into account an array of *affective* factors: How does this student feel about math, about his teacher, and about school in general? What does the teacher know about this student's self-esteem? How does this student relate to the other kids in class? How comfortable is he with taking risks in public? What messages has he received about himself as a learner from his family, from his previous teachers, and from other significant people in his life? Was he in class the day before, and was it a good experience? Or did he miss class and consequently become more self-conscious than in the past?

But that isn't all this teacher needs to consider. What about the student's *cognitive* characteristics? If her job is to help the student to acquire new skills, she needs to know answers to questions such as these: Which of the multiple intelligences are this child's strengths and which are his weaknesses? Does he have a dominant learning style or styles? Has he mastered all of the prerequisite skills, or do developmental gaps exist that will need to be remediated before he can experience success? Does the student learn best when presented material symbolically, or would the use of concrete manipulatives be a more productive strategy for him?

Most of us would agree that it is necessary to consider each of these and dozens of other affective and cognitive factors if a teacher is to succeed in facilitating learning. But teaching isn't even that simple. This student is but one of many in the class. This example, like all lesson planning decisions, involves a complex equation because each child brings to class literally dozens of relevant variables pertaining to his or her emotional and intellectual ability to learn a particular concept. For a class of 30 or more students, the sum of the factors to consider when planning a lesson can be mind-boggling. Perhaps good teachers should consider these thousands of variables when planning a lesson, but it certainly isn't easy.

Nor is that the extent of the challenge. Student characteristics are just a part of the equation. What about all the different teaching strategies and pedagogical approaches that the teacher could consider using? Would this concept (the addition of two-digit numbers) be best taught via lecture, demonstration, exploration, or a hands-on approach? Is the explanation supplied by the textbook satisfactory, or will it need to be supplemented by a practical demonstration employing real-life examples?

Alas, that's not all. A good teacher must have more than pedagogical expertise to design an effective lesson. A competent teacher must also take into account everything known about the subject (mathematics in this case). For example, how could this concept be related to prior and future learnings? What are the essential concepts that need to be derived from this material? Etc., etc., etc.

Without having to devote the rest of the book to this one 2nd grade example, suffice it to say that an extraordinary number of independent variables influence the success of each teaching decision and how that decision ultimately influences each child's learning. Unlike the finite list of factors that the engineer needed to consider in designing the space shuttle, the variables classroom teachers need to consider seem to change randomly and dramatically from day to day and from child to child.

This is not meant to imply that good and effective teaching is impossible, nor does it justify the contention that any approach is as good as any other. Rather, the purpose of this example is to demonstrate that teaching (even the teaching of "basic" elementary school subjects) is an extraordinarily complex process. More important, to succeed with this type of complex decision making requires inquiring practitioners, teachers who are capable of and interested in mastering new types of thinking and decision making and applying them to unique cases on a regular basis.

While the diversity of our student body has grown—ethnically, affectively, and cognitively—a reliance on traditional approaches to lesson planning, the use of data, and curriculum design have hindered our ability to meet individual student needs. The most problematic of these constraints is a phenomenon I call the "tyranny of central tendency."

The Tyranny of Central Tendency

Statisticians use the term *central tendency* to refer to the level of performance exhibited by the majority of a population. Generally, central tendency is thought of as the average performance of a group. The "tyranny of central tendency" arises when it is inferred that every individual in a population ought to be expected to perform as the "average" member of that population. Unfortunately, educators have allowed this type of thinking to influence far too many educational policy decisions. When they do so, it harms the many students who differ in significant ways from the norm.

When we deconstruct many of the propositions recently put forth by educational policymakers, pundits, school administrators, and even a number of teachers, we could easily conclude that today's public school students are much more alike than different. Consider how often we have heard statements such as these:

- Retention harms students.
- The best way to learn math is conceptually.
- Cooperative learning deepens understanding.
- Experiencing logical consequences improves control over behavior.

I, for one, have not only said each of these, but I have truly believed them. The problem is not in what is being said, but what is left unsaid—specifically, the qualifier "for many students." To be accurate, someone—such as I—should be stating:

- Retention is harmful *for many students.*
- *For many students* the best way to learn math is conceptually.
- Cooperative learning can deepen understanding for *many students.*
- Experiencing logical consequences helps *many students* gain control over their behavior.

The tyranny of central tendency becomes harmful whenever policy-makers maintain that a particular practice can work equally well or equally poorly for every student in every circumstance. If this appears to be hairsplitting or an overstatement, consider the practices educators use when adopting materials and curriculums. Aren't these strategies based upon the notion (assumption) that there exists a one best set of materials for all kids? Furthermore, curriculum leaders justify their belief that the materials recommended for adoption are the best for all students by claiming that "research" (statistical tests) supports that conclusion. To understand the problem this creates for the well-intentioned classroom teacher, it is helpful to look at the way research findings and central tendency inform decision making in other professions.

Central Tendency in Medicine vs. Teaching

In recent years I have begun paying closer attention to news reports about medical breakthroughs. (Perhaps this is a sign of my advancing old age). One morning I heard a reporter sharing what he viewed to be an alarming statistic: 15 percent of heavy smokers who began smoking as teenagers will suffer life-shortening illnesses. Although those facts came as no surprise to me, I did a double-take on an aspect of this statistic that the reporter left unsaid—specifically, that 85 percent of heavy smokers who began smoking as teenagers would *not* suffer life-shortening illnesses.

If educators ever came upon a treatment, let's say a reading program, that was effective for 85 percent of the children, they would be so thrilled they would not only quickly adopt it for their school but would advocate its use everywhere. However, it would still cause me to ask about the other 15 percent—those students for whom this "proven" approach to reading wouldn't be successful. Do we just forget about them? If medicine followed that reasoning, teenage smoking would no longer be considered a public health concern, because it only affects a small fraction (15 percent) of the young people who engage in this behavior.

I believe we should continue to be concerned about practices that harm many, even most, children. Following that reasoning, I find myself, for example, in fundamental agreement with those who oppose wholesale retention. I feel justified in this stance because it is clear that most retained students experience far more damage than benefit from this practice. But upon further analysis I have to ask: Does the available research justify a total ban on retention? I would say absolutely not! Such a policy will inevitably hurt some kids, because we know that a small number of students, perhaps as many as 25 percent of those retained, could derive positive results from retention.

Fortunately, our medical colleagues aren't always looking for the "one right answer" for each of the ills afflicting humankind. Rather, they are searching for enough different answers to be able to serve each of the diverse patients who might be suffering from an illness.

Now imagine a parent sending a child to a school that has just adopted the "best available" reading program after a lengthy and rigorous adoption process. This program was proven to be effective with 75 percent of students. Knowing that three out of four students are likely to prosper as a result of the decision to adopt this program is an exciting thought. No one could fault a school board for adopting a program with such powerful evidence behind it.

But before we become too smug about such a decision, it is worth asking: What if the child in question happened to be one of the 25 percent who wouldn't thrive under this program? If these "wonderful proven materials" were adopted, the child's teacher would be forced to use this program with each of the students, including this child. I suspect such a reality would be a significant concern for the parent. In fact, it would bother me every bit as much as having my daughter's pediatrician tell me she was forced to give Emma penicillin even though Emma was allergic to it. It wouldn't make me feel any better if the doctor explained that the reason for prescribing penicillin was that the hospital board had determined it to be the most effective antibiotic on the market and that's why they had "adopted" it. It's hard to imagine any self-respecting doctor wanting to be put in that position, nor would parents want to hear such a justification for an inappropriate medical treatment of their child. It seems reasonable to conclude that if that type of rationale is inappropriate for doctors and their patients, then it should be considered equally inappropriate for teachers and their students.

The focus on central tendency becomes tyrannical whenever it is said that what is good for the majority is, by definition, good for everyone. It becomes unethical when it implies ignoring data on what is appropriate for those who don't fit the norm.

Is there a way out from under the tyranny of central tendency? I will argue that alternatives to this tyranny exist in any accountable and responsible profession. If, for example, my doctor finds that I am allergic to an antibiotic, she doesn't say, "Sorry, that's the one we've adopted; so you'd better take it and like it!" It is far more likely that she will try another medicine that, in her professional judgment, will suit me better. But her efforts don't end there. When she chooses a treatment for me, she collects data to assess the effectiveness of that decision (placing data in my medical records). Then she uses these data on the efficacy of her treatment decisions to inform her next actions. If her hunch regarding the appropriate treatment for me turned out to be wrong, as evidenced by the data collected, she will be the first to learn of that error, giving her a reason to explore other approaches. Because of this pattern of professional behavior, I get quality medical attention tailored to my needs. Equally important, in the process of treating me, my doctor and her colleagues develop increased expertise as a consequence of what they learn from the data on my case.

What I have described applies not only to the world of medicine; it also applies to the world of the teacher action researcher. Whether confronting a problem with an individual student or an issue affecting a broad range of students, "inquiring" teachers use all of their knowledge about each individual and the instructional context, as well as what they can discern from the professional literature, to design appropriate instructional interventions. Furthermore, by collecting data on the effectiveness of each teaching decision, inquiring teachers expand their knowledge base as well as their profession's understanding on how to address similar cases in the future. By looking at each student as an individual case and searching for solutions that make sense for that individual case, teachers can actively resist the tyranny of central tendency and move closer to achieving universal academic success.

The Challenge of Standards-Based Reform

In this chapter I have made several comparisons between teaching and the practice of medicine. Some might argue that making the consequences of the tyranny of central tendency in medicine analogous to the consequences in education is unfair. A critic might say that even if smoking proves harmful for only a relatively small percentage of the population, the harm to those individuals is too great to ignore. Likewise, even if an allergy to penicillin afflicts only a small percentage of patients, the consequence for those people is too severe to ignore. I not only plead guilty to the charge, but also will confess that I used the medical analogy deliberately, because of the emotional impact it would convey. However, I think the analogy is justified.

The current educational policy in effect in most jurisdictions in North America clearly states that schools will be responsible for assisting each student to attain a level of mastery on challenging learning objectives. If these policies merely established a set of ambitious goals with no consequences for not achieving them, it might not be a great source of concern. But the standards movement, as enacted in most jurisdictions, is not just a challenge. Increasingly, policymakers are enacting legislation with high-stakes consequences for the students and schools that fail to achieve mastery on the new standards. Those students who, under current conditions, are unlikely to achieve mastery will pay a price with lifetime consequences. Perhaps it is correct to say that failing to graduate from high school is not as severe a consequence as contracting lung cancer or emphysema, but it is a matter of no small significance.

If teachers are unable to craft instructional interventions that are appropriate not only for the "average" student—that student who falls right in the middle of the distribution—but also for all other students, the impact on children's future lives will be of utmost significance. What happens to children in elementary school can affect their income, job security, mental health, and access to health care for the rest of their lives. It has always been cause for concern when students fail to realize their potential. However, in this era of standards and high-stakes testing, failing to receive educational treatment that is appropriate to one's needs will have consequences beyond what students have ever experienced before.

Meeting the Challenge

The challenge before educators at the start of the 21st century is clear. They are being asked to do what has heretofore been deemed impossible: to assist every child in our diverse student bodies to achieve mastery of a meaningful curriculum. It is an exciting challenge, and there is good reason to believe that the collective wisdom of the education profession is capable of meeting it. But it is equally clear that to succeed, one very important thing needs to change: teaching needs to become a professional pursuit.

If we are to meet the needs of a diverse population and help public education meet its moral goal of providing equal opportunity, then we need to break the tyranny of central tendency and discover an array of instructional techniques appropriate for even the smallest subpopulation of learners. To accomplish this, we need a teaching force armed with data that they can use to make the pursuit of continuous improvement a normal part of school life.

I am not so naive as to think that one simple seven-step process will save the entire enterprise of public education, but I have witnessed schools where high-efficacy teachers are making breakthroughs and producing data on the impact of those breakthroughs on student performance. I've listened as teacher researchers share their insights, and I've noticed that each report is like a pebble thrown in a pond. The ripples created become bigger and reach far beyond the place of entry. That is why I believe it is a most propitious time to become engaged in making teaching the fulfilling profession it needs and deserves to be.

The next sections of the book return to the practical issues of how to conduct action research (individually, collaboratively, and as part of a schoolwide improvement effort) and how to institutionalize teacher inquiry as a normative aspect of school life. Beginning in Chapter 5, we examine in depth how action research can be used to attack complex teaching challenges. The examination focuses on two related issues in reading. The first, encapsulated in the question "How might a teacher improve the inferential comprehension of their students?" is the type of issue that often concerns an individual classroom teacher. The second, summarized in the question "How can we improve the reading performance of our students on the state proficiency exam?" is the type of issue that might concern an entire school.

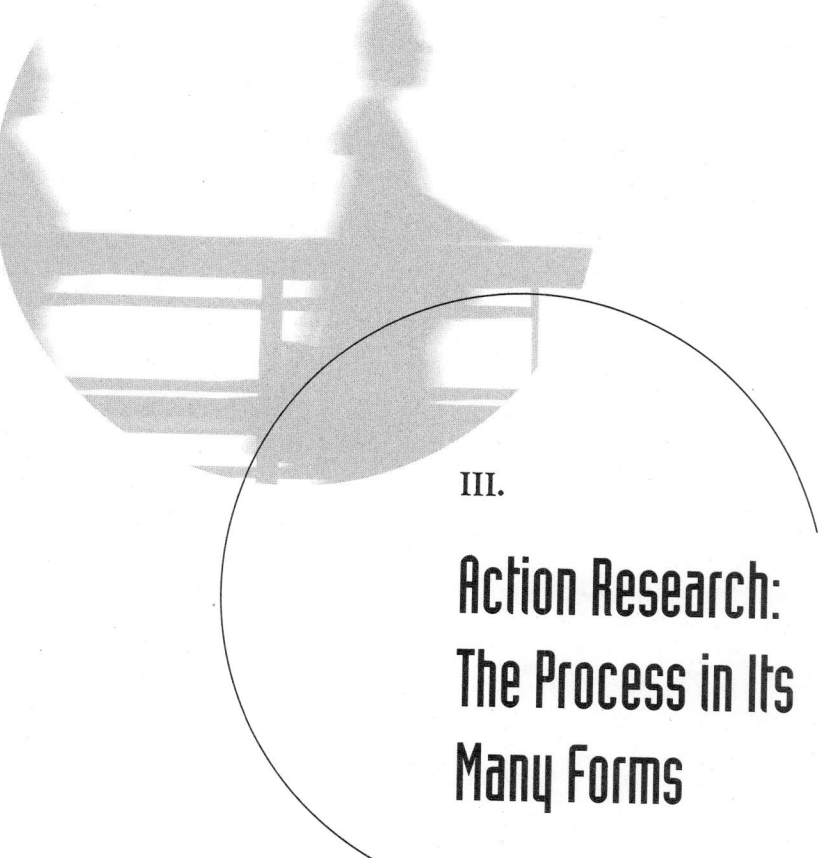

III.

Action Research: The Process in Its Many Forms

5 Choosing the Right Research Questions and Assessment Criteria

I hope that by now you have decided to explore making inquiry, experimentation, and action research part of your professional routine. If so, you are about to embark on an exciting journey. Michael Fullan (1991) aptly notes that "change is a journey, not a destination." This is always the case when engaging in action research. Because of the complexity of the teaching and learning process, it is impossible to predict, with any degree of certainty, where inquiries will ultimately lead.

It is important to inquire into an issue or study a phenomenon that is particularly relevant to your work. In fact, the personal relevance of the topic is an essential prerequisite when choosing an action research focus. At Project LEARN[1] my colleagues and I developed a flexible position on what constitutes an appropriate focus for teacher research. Project LEARN participants were told that an appropriate action research topic ought to meet three criteria:

- It involves an issue within the scope of the researcher's authority. (Functionally this means it pertains to teaching and learning.)
- It is a matter that the educator is personally and passionately concerned about.
- It involves a matter on which student or teacher performance could and should be improved.

---

[1]Project LEARN (League of Educational Action Researchers in the Northwest) is a Washington State University program. The processes used in Project LEARN are detailed in *How to Conduct Collaborative Action Research* (Sagor, 1993).

This chapter will explore "topic generation" by looking specifically at how middle school teachers might attack the following questions (both of which meet the criteria listed above):

Individual Teacher Question: How might I improve the inferential comprehension of my students?

Schoolwide Question: How can we improve the reading performance of our students on the state proficiency exam?

Chapters 1 and 2 introduced the seven steps of the action research process. Here I present specific instructions—implementation strategies—for using each of the techniques described. For example, Chapter 2 described how a teacher could use a journal to find a focus for research. What follows is a more thorough discussion of keeping a journal, accompanied by the first implementation strategy.

Keeping a Journal

To explain the value of this strategy, I return to my favorite analogy—the primary care physician. Although contemporary doctors don't work under all of the constraints of the typical educator, their workdays are, nevertheless, marked by a fragmentation that most teachers could empathize with. In the realm of individual differences, most primary care physicians work with caseloads perhaps more diverse than that of an urban classroom teacher. The following is a typical slice of life for a primary care physician.

The day begins in Room 1, where the doctor attends to an elderly patient with heart trouble. In Room 2, the next patient is an 8-year old boy who is combating a persistent weight problem. Then it is on to Room 3 and a middle-aged construction worker who requires treatment for painful muscle spasms. After a day of examining and treating 25 to 30 individual patients, responding by phone to inquiries from another dozen patients, resolving some office personnel problems, and conducting rounds at the hospital, the doctor is finally ready to go home. In all likelihood, the doctor's life at this point seems even more disjointed and out of control than the life of the typical classroom teacher.

I've often wondered why doctors seem to know patients so well in the office and be so aware of the specifics of their cases, yet barely recognize them when they pass them on the street. Why is this? What is it that helps my doctor maintain focus in the midst of this tornado of patient diversity? Paraphrasing a political cliché, "It's the records, stupid!"

After seeing a patient, doctors generally retreat to a private office where they can dictate their impressions, actions, concerns, and expectations into recording equipment conveniently located on the desk. Barring a crisis of some sort, the doctor probably won't return to this material until minutes before the patient's next visit. However, with even a cursory review of past trends, updated by data surfaced during the exam, and by probing with a few focused questions, a good doctor is not only able to observe patterns in a patient's medical condition, but is able to suggest a set of appropriate next steps for the patient's care.

Perhaps we should consider issuing teachers dictating machines and invite them to dictate their impressions following each day's classes. They could use this equipment to detail perceptions, interventions, and pertinent discussions held with students and colleagues. They could drop the tapes off for transcription before leaving school each afternoon. Office staff, working the night shift, could then transcribe the tapes and post the remarks onto the teachers' working files for the student being discussed. What teacher wouldn't love to have a detailed, running record of each child's academic performance (dictated in the teacher's own words), produced over the course of a full academic year, to use when preparing for a parent conference?

Just as the notes in a patient's file can help the physician spot trends (positive or negative) regarding a patient's response to the treatment regime, the examination of a variety of patient files (all from individuals suffering from the same condition) gives the inquiring physician a chance to observe patterns or trends that cut across patients. The very act of keeping a journal does the same thing for the classroom teacher. For this and many other reasons, keeping a teaching journal has proven to be a real asset for many teacher researchers.

Perhaps you already have the journal habit. Or perhaps, like me, you are not so sure you are interested in committing to another (potentially time-consuming) habit. Don't worry—a commitment to keeping a journal needn't be forever. To get started with teacher research, you might consider keeping a journal for a few weeks. Doing so for even a brief time is a way to productively surface and refine an action research focus.

Implementation Strategy #1—Using a Teaching Journal to Find an Action Research Focus

WHAT:
A process for finding an issue or issues important enough to become the focus for action research

HOW:
1. Pledge (to yourself or to teammates) to write for a minimum of 10 minutes in a "researcher's journal" each afternoon immediately after students leave the classroom. Continue to do so for two weeks.

2. Decide on a prompt for journal reflections. (Do this with teammates if this is a group effort.) The prompt might be a generic question such as "What happened in class today that was particularly interesting, exciting, frustrating, or fun?" or it could be a more focused question such as "What happened in class today *pertaining to reading* that was particularly frustrating?"

3. After two weeks, reread your journal to reflect on what, if any, patterns or themes emerged. (If this is group work, everyone attends a meeting to share their reflections.) The patterns that surface could include concerns, priorities, frustrations, dreams, and so on. When doing this exercise alone, it is helpful to discuss your journal with a trusted colleague or friend to help you identify trends.

4. Review the list of patterns or themes. When doing this as a group it is a good idea to write the themes prominently on a piece of chart paper for everyone to see and consider before discussing them as potential foci for action research. Then open the meeting for questions to clarify what is actually meant by each theme.

5. If working individually, ask yourself, "Do I wish to pursue action research on any of these themes, patterns, or trends?" If working as a collegial team, ask, "Does anyone on this team wish to investigate any of these themes, patterns, or trends?" If the answer to either question is yes, you have found a potential action research focus or set of foci. If the answer is no, repeat the process until a focus stimulates professional concern or enthusiasm.

Keeping a journal is a good technique, but it is not the only way to choose an action research focus. Another related approach, increasingly favored by teacher researchers, involves the use of the Internet for collegial reflection. Posting questions to teacher bulletin boards and list-serves is an increasingly popular way to engage colleagues in a reflective dialogue. I subscribe to several list-serves that are frequented by teacher researchers from around the world. It is not at all uncommon to read a posting from a teacher asking for assistance with a classroom issue. The e-mail responses that follow often surface many viable foci for action research.

Engaging in Dialogue

Another mechanism that helps when searching your teaching soul for a research focus is far "lower tech" than the Internet. It involves engaging a colleague in a one-on-one dialogue over issues of concern regarding teaching. Chapter 1 introduced the process of the reflective interview.

Implementation Strategy #2—The Reflective Interview

WHAT: A process for surfacing topics worthy of becoming potential foci for action research

HOW:

1. Choose an interview partner. It is not important that the partner share your teaching assignment or, for that matter, that you even work in the same school. All that matters is that this person is an educator who can listen well and is likely to understand what you have to say.

2. Choose the topic for your 20-minute part of the interview. (Your partner should also choose a topic.) Your interview topic (for the purpose of surfacing action research topics) should conform to an agreed upon prompt. Prompts can range from the general (for example, the topic must concern teaching and/or learning; it must be a matter of significant concern to you; the condition could be improved by your actions) to the specific (for example, the topic must concern reading; student performance could be improved by your actions).

3. Follow these rules for the interview:

• The interviewee is the talker. Imagine that an invisible time-keeper is tracking the use of air time. After 20 minutes, the timekeeper's records should indicate that the interviewee was talking at least 90 percent of the time.

• The interviewer is to refrain from offering suggestions, stating opinions, and making judgments. Instead the interviewer's role is to ask clarifying questions and to help the interviewee explore his or her own thinking on the issue.

4. Flip a coin to see who will go first. Then begin the first interview.

5. After 20 minutes, reverse roles. For the next 20 minutes the person who played the role of interviewer becomes the interviewee.

6. At the end of your interview, ask yourself, "Was the issue I discussed truly worth investing my time researching?" If you answer yes, you've found a focus. If not, repeat the process with other topics until one surfaces that interests you enough to justify its investigation.

Setting Targets

My good friend Rick Stiggins, the assessment guru and author of *Student-Centered Classroom Assessment* (1994), has often said, "Any student can hit any target, provided the student is able to see the target and the target agrees to stand still long enough!" The same could be said for teacher action researchers.

Choosing a focus for teacher research is a necessary, but not sufficient, first step. This is because choosing a target and seeing that target clearly can be two very different things. Generally the focus for action research pertains to student achievement—for example, improving creative writing skills, developing self-discipline, or enhancing problem-solving skills in mathematics. In other cases, the research focus relates to a teaching technique—for example, teaching to multiple intelligences, managing an inclusive classroom, or determining elements of productive peer teaching.

At the start of this chapter I presented two questions that could frame an issue or a topic for action research related to improvement of reading. The question for an individual researcher framed the issue as improving the inferential comprehension of his or her students. The schoolwide question dealt with the issue of improving the reading performance of a large group of students on the state proficiency exam.

Whatever the issue being studied, it is always worthwhile to spend some time clarifying the targets, or desired outcomes, before proceeding. As Stiggins says, if we are to hit a target, it is essential that we be able to see it. This is why it is important to state precisely and unambiguously exactly what it is you wish to accomplish. The value of this maxim applies not only to action research but also to how we use our discretionary time away from the classroom. For example, when I make an appointment with a golf pro to help straighten out my drive, it is important for both the pro and me to know precisely what I want to accomplish and what criteria we will use to judge my performance. Neither the pro nor I wish to waste valuable time on tangential issues.

Setting clear achievement targets does more than just keep a person on track. With a clear target in mind, constructing credible assessments becomes much easier. In relation to the academic issue at hand (improving student reading), articulating clear and unambiguous targets at the onset of research will enable an objective assessment of how close the researchers have come and are coming to hitting their targets.

In traditional experimental research, measurements of proximity to a target are called measures of the treatment effect on the *dependent variable*. Measurements of a dependent variable inform the researcher about the power of the intervention. Therefore, to get a sense of how successful a particular teaching technique was in achieving your goal (target), you first need to clarify and be able to articulate precisely what your target looks like. This must happen well before the intervention is introduced (ideally, it should occur even before you plan the intervention). In the final analysis, the success claimed for any intervention must be based upon credible and measurable impact on the target.

The Rating Scale: A Mechanism for Measuring the Dependent Variable

Teachers don't acquire teaching skills and develop their knowledge all at once. The same is true of student learning. Few valued goals are ever attained in one fell swoop. This explains why an investigation of student progress in reading is rarely framed in terms of whether a student *can* or *cannot* comprehend. It is much more common to speak of a learner's *relative* proficiency with comprehension. For example, a narrative evaluation might contain the comment that a student "can accurately paraphrase facts from his reading but still has difficulty drawing inferences." Similarly, an assessor wouldn't say a teacher can or cannot teach reading. More likely, assessment comments would focus on a teacher's skill with a particular instructional technique.

In most states and provinces the state board of education or education ministry has adopted or is in the process of adopting content standards. Content standards are statements of skills that policymakers contend should be achieved by students as a result of schooling. A typical content standard might sound like this: By the end of 8th grade, all students will be able to read and understand general circulation newspapers.

Now let's assume I am a teacher who wants to investigate my efforts at helping students improve their reading comprehension. Furthermore, let's assume that my motivation to work on this is to enable my students to demonstrate proficiency on the specific content standard referred to above.

When I discuss defining and articulating achievement targets, I find that archery provides a useful analogy. The primary goal of any archer is to consistently have the arrows hit the target. Yet, most archers hope that over time they will be able not only to hit the target but also to strike ever closer to the bull's-eye. Declaring a general focus for action research is the same as announcing that I am aiming my arrows toward the target. The archery target is the content standard; so in this case my chosen target is "the reading and understanding of general circulation newspapers." But simply making that statement does not provide me with enough clarity to make meaningful assessments.

Like the archer, I know there is a wide range of performances that could qualify as hitting the target (comprehending newspapers). Furthermore, I realize that it will require more from me (and from my students) to achieve at the higher levels of comprehension (the bull's-eye) than to simply demonstrate minimal proficiency. If my research is to be sensitive to distinctions in performance, it is imperative that I, the researcher, clarify for myself (and when appropriate, for others) how I will determine the difference between a bull's-eye and simply "adequate" performance. Just as archers use numbers to score their shooting, teachers often do the same. Applying numbers to distinguish among levels of performance is the purpose of what is popularly called a "nominal scoring guide," a "rating scale," or a "rubric."

In my effort to enhance my students' comprehension of general circulation newspapers, I might develop this scoring guide:

5 = The student is able to explain the point of view of the author and make reasoned judgments on the author's position on related topics.

4 = The student can demonstrate an understanding of the author's point of view and is able to cite portions of the text that convey that point of view.

3 = The student understands the main ideas in the article and can restate those ideas in his or her own words.

2 = The student understands the main idea and can point out where in the text that idea is conveyed.

1 = The student has a general idea of the thrust of the article.

Although I might feel confident in arguing that any student whose work hit the target (a score of 1, 2, 3, 4, or 5) did in fact demonstrate comprehension of a general circulation newspaper article, I would agree that a student whose work consistently scored at a 5 level had demonstrated this academic skill far more powerfully than a classmate who scored a 1. Later, when as an action researcher I begin analyzing student performance data, it will be useful to analyze the distribution of the arrows (student performance) on the target (the scoring guide) over time. As a researcher, I will want to compare and contrast student scores both before and after my instructional intervention. The ultimate distribution of student scores on the scoring guide or rubric will provide me with some significant insights into the success of the strategies I employed.

Once I have established assessment criteria, it is time for me to start conducting research on my development (in this case, as a teacher of inferential comprehension). As the school year progresses, I will be able to monitor my progress. With the aid of my rating scale (rubric), I will not only be able to answer whether I did well, but I will be able to state specifically how well I did.

Implementation Strategy #3—Setting Targets: Defining Criteria to Measure the Dependent Variable

WHAT:
Setting criteria to assess the impact of instruction

HOW:
1. With a partner, discuss your general goal (e.g., student motivation, problem-solving skills, self-discipline,) until you reach a shared understanding of your target.

2. Discuss the observable behaviors or performances that you hope to produce. Make sure your descriptors are discrete, unambiguous, and easily understood. Assign this performance a score of 3.

3. Discuss and agree on the *minimum* descriptor, behavior, or performance you could accept as a demonstration of this skill. Select descriptors that are discrete, unambiguous, and easily understood. Assign this performance a score of 1.

4. Discuss and agree on a behavior or performance that you would consider an *exemplary* demonstration of this skill. Select descriptors that are discrete, unambiguous, and easily understood. Assign this performance a score of 5.

5. Discuss and agree on behaviors or performances you might observe that fall incrementally between the ones you've already identified. Select descriptors of those performances that are concise, unambiguous, and easily understood. Assign these performances scores of 2 and 4.

6. Share and discuss the scoring guides that emerged with your colleague(s). This step will help you ascertain if the descriptors and rating criteria are clear and if educators hold a consensus on their appropriateness as measures.

7. Once agreement has been reached, pat yourself on the back. You have just produced a rating scale that will help you measure the success of your efforts on your "dependent variable."

Figure 5.1 (p. 58) is an example of a rating scale that a teacher might use for measuring success with improving the inferential reading comprehension of 7th grade students.

Figure 5.2 (p. 59) is an example of a rating scale that might be developed by a faculty wishing to improve the performance of its entire student body (including each racial, ethnic, and gender subgroup) on the reading portion of a state proficiency exam.

Once you have identified a focus for your action research and have developed a rating scale (rubric) that will help you assess your progress, you are ready to move to the second stage of the action research process—clarifying your theory or theories. Chapter 6 examines in depth a set of strategies that can help you clarify theoretical perspectives on the instructional actions that might improve your teaching and, ultimately, student learning.

FIGURE 5.1

Rating Scale
Improving Inferential Comprehension

BASIC 1	2	DEVELOPING 3	4	FLUENT 5
After reading a grade level-appropriate essay, the student can accurately restate the main idea.	After reading a grade-level-appropriate essay, the student can accurately retell the author's thesis.	After reading a grade-level-appropriate essay, the student can accurately retell and support the author's thesis with multiple details from the text.	After reading a grade-level-appropriate essay, the student can accurately retell and support the author's thesis with multiple details from the text and can draw logical inferences about the author's point of view.	After reading a grade-level-appropriate essay, the student can accurately retell and support the author's thesis with multiple details from the text, draw logical inferences about the author's point of view, and persuasively support those inferences by referencing the language and vocabulary used by the author.

FIGURE 5.2

Rating Scale
Improving Reading Performance on the State Test

BASIC 1	2	SATISFACTORY 3	4	EXEMPLARY 5
Each of the (demographic) subgroups that had scored below the 50th percentile on the reading portion of the state test demonstrates statistically significant improvement in reading.	*All* demographic subgroups, regardless of prior performance, demonstrate statistically significant improvement on the reading portion of the state test.	The scores of each demographic subgroup on the reading portion of the state test exceed the 50th percentile.	The scores of each demographic subgroup on the reading portion of the state test exceed the 62nd percentile.	The scores of each demographic subgroup on the reading portion of the state test exceed the 75th percentile.

6 Using Theory to Drive Action

Chapter 5 discussed the importance of setting clear and differentiated achievement targets. Clarifying our targets provides us with precise information about our intended destination.

I travel a great deal, and one thing I take for granted is that the airline I'm traveling on and the pilot who is directing the aircraft share an understanding of our destination (we might call that the plane's achievement target). But knowing a plane's destination is just the starting point. It isn't enough to get it there.

This brings me to a story I frequently share at the beginning of an action research workshop. I tell the participants a scary (although fictitious) story that I contend happened to me the evening before. I relate how anxious I became when the pilot announced that we were returning to the gate because he "didn't like the sound of the starboard engine." I then tell my audience about how this anxiety later turned into abject horror when, after a 10-minute stop at the gate, we were cleared for takeoff. As soon as the "fasten seat belt" light went off, I quizzed the flight attendant about the situation, asking, "What could the airline have possibly done in a mere 10 minutes to fix this problem?" Without missing a beat the attendant responded, "Oh, it was easy. We simply changed pilots."

I use this story to drive home a key point that every reflective educator must be ever cognizant of: the inextricable connection between *theory* and *action*. The specific strategy employed to deal with the problem of an engine emitting a strange sound is determined by whatever theory the pilot holds regarding the source of the problem. Often more than one theory can possess "face validity" as an explanation for a phenomenon. In the case of engine noise, possible explanations might include the following: something was wrong with the pilot's hearing; a window was inadvertently left open; something was mechanically wrong with the starboard engine.

Depending upon the theory held, drastically different actions would be called for, ranging from the simple closing of a window to the grounding of the plane until the engine could be serviced.

As a rule, when actions are taken in accordance with an incorrect or inadequate theory, the underlying problem continues to fester. In the case of my story, if the underlying problem was, in reality, a faulty engine, the consequence of acting in accordance with an incorrect theory could be catastrophic (hence the polite but nervous laughter when I tell this joke).

This same phenomenon, "theory driving action," exists in all the sciences and holds a great deal of meaning for educators. In the past, when educators failed in their best efforts to serve children, it was rarely because of a lack of caring, commitment, or concern. On the contrary, history shows that educational shortcomings have almost always been the result of educators faithfully following theories that later turned out to be incorrect or inadequate.

Failures due to theoretical flaws are normal and expected in the natural sciences, and even in the fields of applied science, such as medicine. Fortunately for scientists, when they fail it seldom results in slanderous charges regarding the scientist's commitment, sincerity, or morality. Unfortunately for educators, when society uncovers a shortfall in school performance, the discovery is often accompanied by a condemnation of the teachers, the schools, or both. How often have you heard shortcomings in student performance asserted to be evidence of teacher incompetence—or worse, callousness? This is a maddening state of affairs for caring teachers for two reasons. First, the teachers whose students underperformed because of the inadequacy of an adopted theory usually feel as bad as the "rock throwers." And, second, the theory that the board of education or the state department of education mandated in all likelihood didn't originate with the implementing teachers. More likely, it originated with a persuasive consultant whose work in the state was underwritten by a lobbyist with an ax to grind.

Clarifying Your Theory

After you have selected a topic that relates to teaching and learning and which you are enthusiastic about pursuing, the next step in the action research process is to clarify your theory. Undoubtedly you (and perhaps some colleagues who have chosen to work with you) already hold a theory or theories on why things have been working out the way they have and what changes would occur if you altered your actions in one way or another. However, perhaps you haven't spent adequate time explicitly and publicly detailing your theoretical perspective. For a variety of reasons, it is important that you do just that before proceeding any further with your research.

One of the best ways to clarify theories and share your assumptions about them is to draw a visual depiction of your thinking. Visual depictions of theories by action researchers are called "graphic reconstructions." In Chapter 2, Figure 2.2 presented an example of a graphic reconstruction developed to illustrate my understanding of the purpose and function of peer editing in the development of middle school writers.

To illuminate how graphic reconstructions are developed and used by teachers working as a collaborative team, let's look at a problem being faced by a hypothetical team of 8th grade social studies teachers. (The hypothetical case being introduced here is actually a composite of work done by a number of teacher researchers.)

When interviewing each other using the reflective interview process (Implementation Strategy #2), Richard and Georgia were surprised, but pleased to find that they shared similar concerns—specifically, their students' apathy about social issues, their alienation from social institutions, and their negative view of politics in general. What concerned these teachers wasn't so much the apathy expressed by their students, but the deep hopelessness that they detected simmering below the surface.

The more these teachers talked, both during and after the reflective interview, the more they began to feel that they understood the issue they were dealing with. They labeled the problem as one of "low social efficacy." This phenomenon resulted, or so they believed, from a deep feeling on the part of many of their kids that middle school students are powerless to change things, be it in their homes, their school, or the larger community. Once this insight surfaced, Richard and Georgia realized they needed to spend some time clarifying the specific achievement target they wanted to see their students succeed with. To do this they enlisted colleagues (teachers from other disciplines) in a process of discussing "social efficacy" as a target and in the creation of a scoring guide/rubric to help assess the school's effectiveness in helping students hit the target.

The faculty at this hypothetical school, High Point Middle School, used Implementation Strategy #3 (see page 56) to create a workable scoring guide/rubric. They believed that having the faculty agree on a performance continuum that could then be used to measure social efficacy would make it easier to design instructional strategies that would likely help students acquire that attribute. The scoring guide/rubric that resulted from their work is illustrated in Figure 6.1.

At this point Richard and Georgia were confident that they knew with some degree of precision what they were seeking to accomplish: students performing at a 3 or better on their school's social efficacy scoring guide. The task now before these teachers was to develop a theory on what could be done to close the gap between their students' current low level of performance on the social efficacy target and the higher levels of social efficacy they desired. Before proceeding any further, Richard and Georgia decided it was time to make a detailed map—a graphic reconstruction—of their theory. After several hours of dialogue, they drew a picture, or graphic reconstruction, of their concern, illustrated in Figure 6.2 (p. 66).

Building this graphic reconstruction (using Post-it notes, chart paper, and colored pens) was a valuable experience. Although it took them several hours to complete the process, once they were done they believed they had created a useful and concrete representation of their theory. Furthermore, the finished graphic enabled them to see that they truly shared a similar perspective on this problem. For example, both teachers believed that the students at High Point felt that adults neither wanted to hear what the students had to say, nor wished to involve students in problem solving.

Richard and Georgia believed that these attitudes contributed to the students' seeing social studies (particularly the study of government) to be little more than a chore that had to be endured. They saw the class as having no real purpose beyond the mere acquisition of credit. As a result of this analysis and further discussion, Richard and Georgia began to see a way out. They called their emerging solution the Real World Advocacy Project, or RWAP, and they created a second graphic reconstruction (Figure 6.3, p. 67) to depict the key components of their theoretical solution.

The RWAP would be a long-term group project that engaged students in researching and taking action on a social issue of personal concern. Richard and Georgia didn't just want their students to study social issues; they wanted them actively engaged in the process of finding solutions to social problems and, hopefully, experiencing the feeling of empowerment that is the birthright of citizens in democracies. The more they worked, the more they began to fall in love with the RWAP idea. It not only was "their baby," but it made perfect sense in light of their

FIGURE 6.1

Rubric for Measuring Social Efficacy

BASIC 1	2	DEVELOPING 3	4	FLUENT 5
Student can express personal opinions about social issues but believes that influencing social change is probably beyond his or her control.	Student can explain personal positions on social issues and expresses confidence that change can occur but is still unsure about his or her potential role in the change process.	Student demonstrates personal commitment to positions on social issues and attempts to influence change by articulately advocating support for positions.	Student's commitment to social issues is demonstrated by engaging in deliberate actions designed to influence policy-makers and decision makers.	Student's commitment to social issues is demonstrated through the strategizing of alternative means to bring about desired change. Student will persevere when and if his or her initial strategies don't prove fruitful.

theory. When they added the RWAP to their map, they felt their graphic reconstruction was complete. The final product (Figure 6.4, p. 68) was a valuable tool for Richard and Georgia. Not only did it help guide their research, but it enabled them to share with students, parents, and colleagues the rationale for introducing the RWAP project and why they felt this strategy held promise for ameliorating the social efficacy problem.

Implementation Strategy #4 details the steps to follow to produce a map of your "implicit theory." The graphic reconstruction that will result should communicate both the intent and rationale for instruction.

Implementation Strategy #4—Building a Graphic Reconstruction

WHO:
Any teacher or group of teachers interested in studying a particular phenomenon.

WHAT:
A process for clarifying beliefs and assumptions regarding a phenomenon.

HOW:
1. Brainstorm every important factor, issue, or variable that relates to the problem about which you are concerned.

2. Write each of the factors, issues, or variables on a separate Post-it note.

3. Using a large piece of poster paper, rearrange the Post-it notes in a manner that helps illustrate the problem you are concerned with as well as the theoretical solution(s) you hope to pursue.

4. Decide if you fundamentally agree with the depiction of the phenomenon as illustrated on your map.

5. If your answer to the above is yes, your graphic representation is complete. If not, repeat the process until you are confident that it represents your best thinking.

FIGURE 6.2

Graphic Reconstruction of Problem

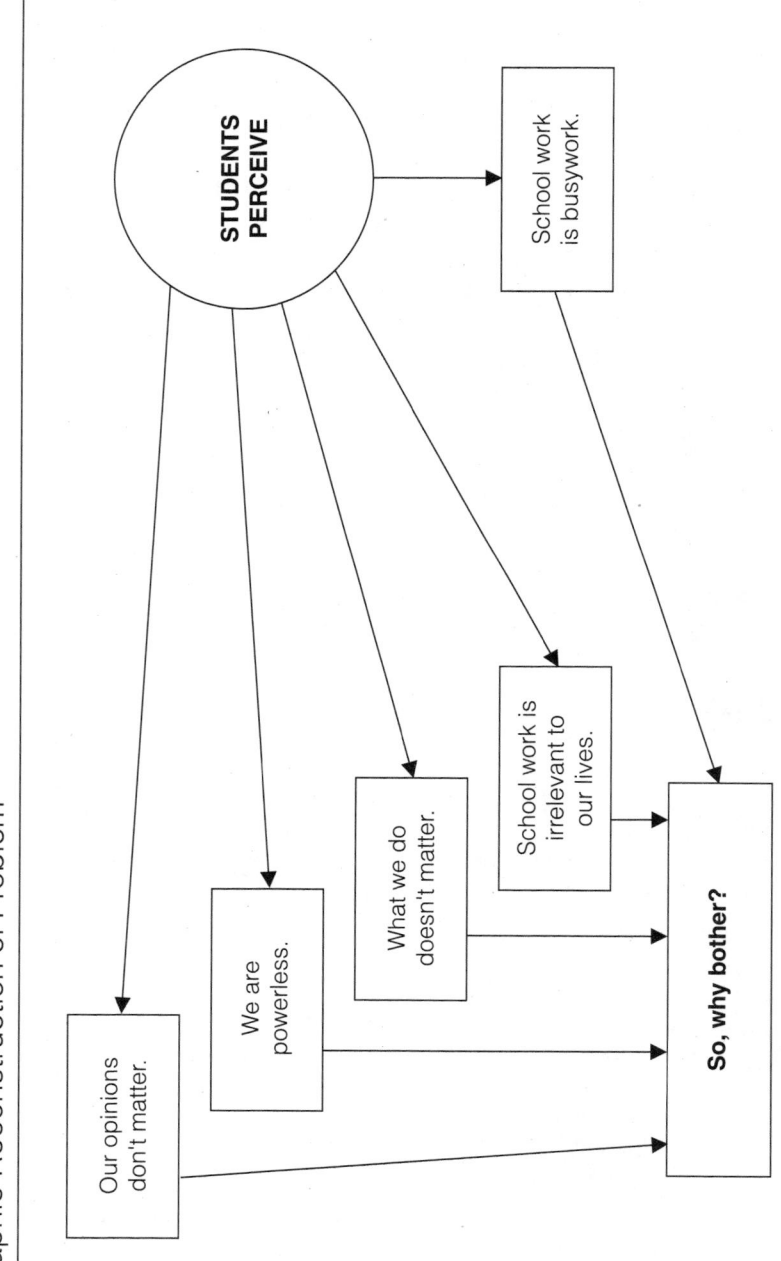

FIGURE 6.3

Graphic Reconstruction of a Possible Solution

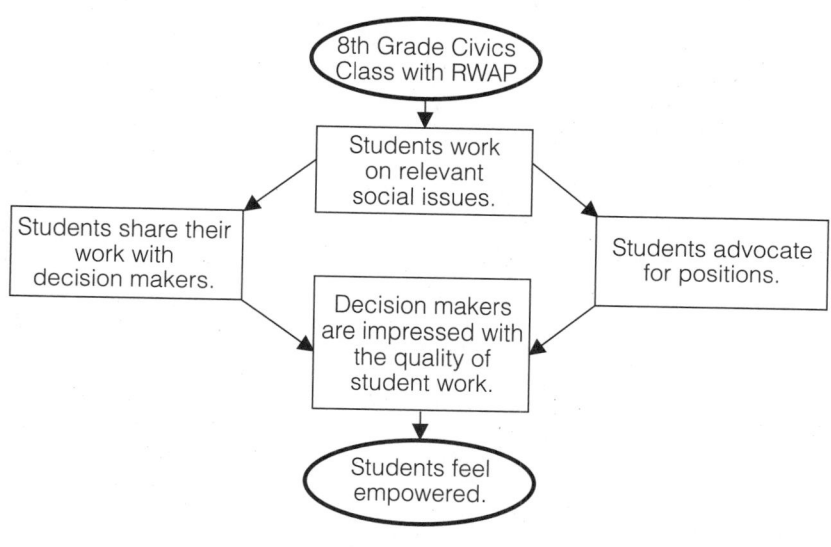

For professionals intent on employing logical, thoughtful, and reasoned approaches to solving problems, developing a visual map that faithfully describes one's theoretical perspectives and proposals for improvement can be a major accomplishment in itself. Engaging in a reflective dialogue on an issue and then illustrating the analysis visually are strategies that work for almost any proposal for program improvement. In many situations, the program planning process is considered adequate and complete once an agreed upon graphic reconstruction has been developed.

However, when plowing what is essentially new ground, it isn't enough to simply propose interventions that are well thought through and logical. This is because even a logical theory is still a "hunch" or, in scientific terms, a working hypothesis about what one *thinks* or *believes* is going on and what one posits will ultimately improve things. So although you might feel good about a proposed plan of action and the theory that informs it (as illustrated in your graphic reconstructions), you still need to find evidence regarding whether your hypothesis is correct or not and why.

Figure 6.4
Graphic Reconstruction of Action Plan

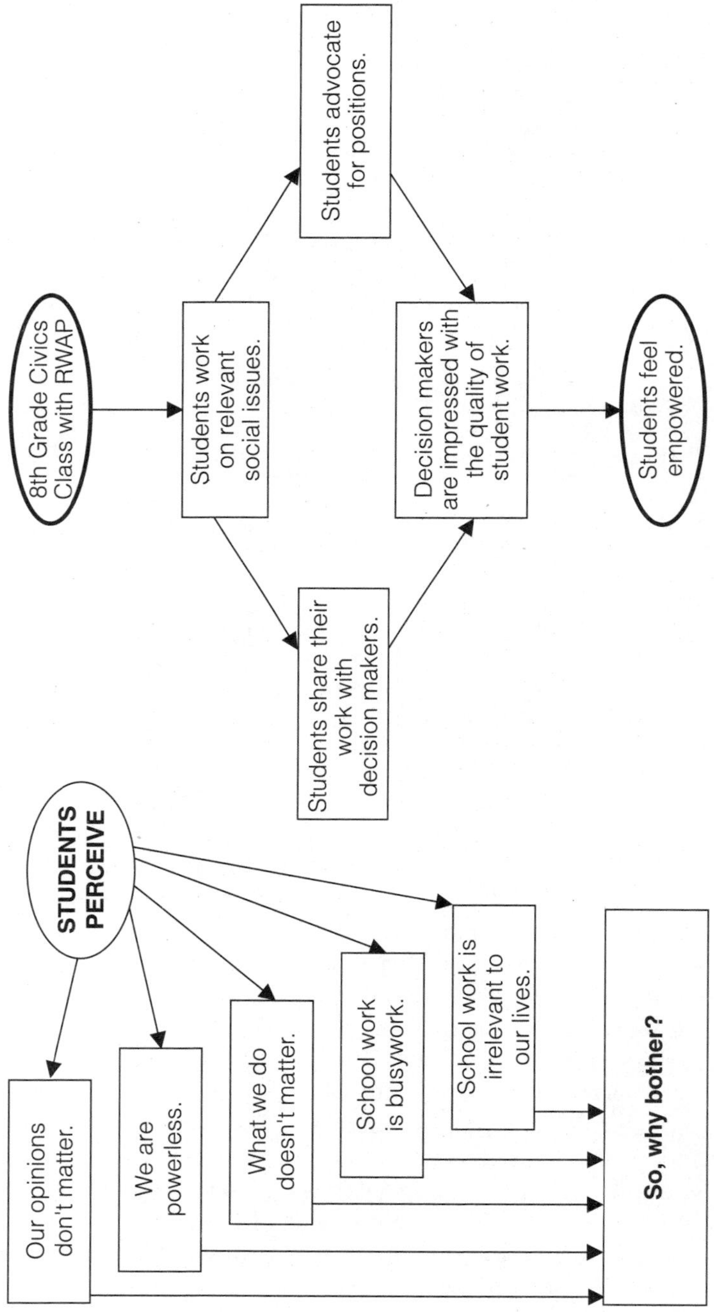

8th Grade Civics Class with RWAP

Students work on relevant social issues.

Students advocate for positions.

Students share their work with decision makers.

Decision makers are impressed with the quality of student work.

Students feel empowered.

STUDENTS PERCEIVE

Our opinions don't matter.

We are powerless.

What we do doesn't matter.

School work is busywork.

School work is irrelevant to our lives.

So, why bother?

As an action researcher, you simultaneously wear two hats, that of actor and researcher. The graphic reconstruction is what the actor needs. It tell the "actor" the steps to follow. But as a researcher, you need something more; you need valid and reliable data to answer questions regarding the appropriateness of your actions. So as the actor in you gets ready to implement your chosen strategy (the RWAP project in Richard and Georgia's case), the researcher in you needs to identify the specific research questions that are worth investing time and energy to investigate.

Surfacing Research Questions

The best way to surface specific questions is through a disciplined and thoughtful examination of the theory illustrated in your graphic reconstruction. The way to accomplish this is with the "two-step test."

Implementation Strategy #5—Analyzing the Graphic Reconstruction with the Two-Step Test

WHAT:
A process for isolating research questions worthy of further exploration

HOW:
1. Take out your graphic reconstruction and ask yourself (or the members of your group) if you believe this map still depicts your best thinking on the phenomenon. If the answer is yes, you are ready to proceed. If not, repeat Implementation Strategy #4.

2. Understand that every aspect of the map is no more than an assumption. Recognize that the clustering of variables, the arrows flowing from one variable to another, the relationships between variables, even speculation on the existence of the variables are assumptions as to what constitutes reality.

3. Determine the importance of each variable, relationship, or factor illustrated on your graphic reconstruction. Do this by asking the following question of each variable, factor, or relationship: *Is this variable, factor, or relationship significant?* Put a letter S by each factor, relationship, or variable that you feel is a matter of more than passing significance. Items

that don't receive the S designation are thus deemed to lack enough significance to merit further investigation.

4. Determine how much confidence you have in your hunches and assumptions. Look at each factor, variable, or relationship that was deemed significant enough to justify research (that received an S designation) and ask yourself: *How confident or certain am I/are we about this assumption?* Next to each factor that you or your teaching partners feel more than a little uncertain about, place a U.

5. Now list all of the factors, relationships, or variables that received designations of S *and* U. These are aspects of your theory that you both deem significant and that you feel merit further study because of your uncertainty.

6. Prepare a list of tentative research questions responding to those issues that you marked with an S *and* a U.

The two-step test is based on an understanding that everything on your graphic reconstruction is an assumption or a hunch until evidence tells you otherwise. In addition, this process recognizes that your time and energy are limited. This is why, before proceeding to data collection, you want to ask two critical questions regarding every assumption on your graphic representation: Is this factor, variable, or relationship significant? Am I/are we relatively uncertain about this factor, variable, or relationship?

You do this because whether it is factual or not, if a relationship isn't significant, it is unreasonable to waste finite time investigating it. Similarly, if you are already certain about a relationship, you might just be reinventing the wheel if you investigate it further. The two-step test helps isolate questions that focus on significant relationships that arouse reasonable uncertainty.

Figure 6.5 shows the final graphic reconstruction prepared by Georgia and Richard marked with S's and U's. The notations show that these action researchers felt that the following factors and relationships were significant:

- Students feel that their opinions don't matter.
- Students feel that they are powerless.
- Students feel that schoolwork is busywork.
- Students see schoolwork as largely irrelevant to their lives.

FIGURE 6.5

Graphic Reconstruction of Action Research Problem

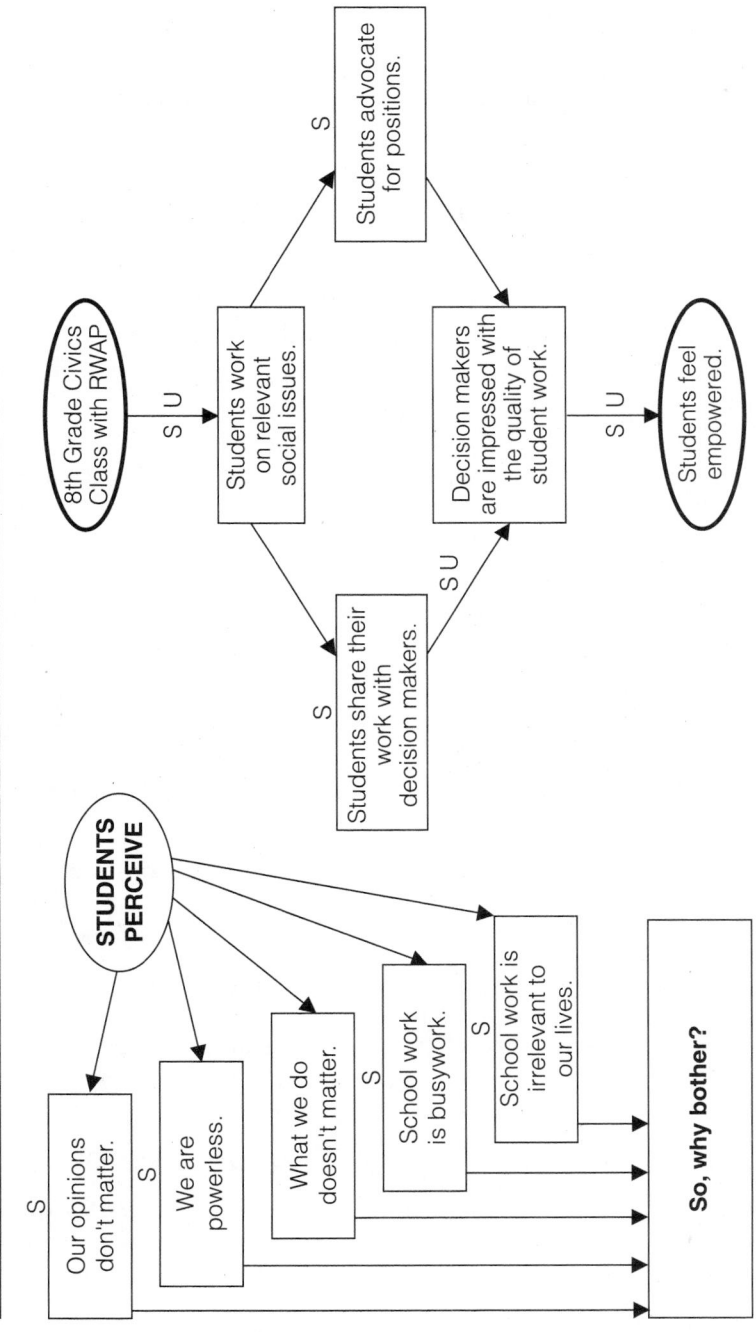

- Students should work on relevant social issues.
- Students need to share their work with decision makers.
- Students should advocate for positions.
- Decision makers are impressed with the quality of student work.
- Sharing ideas and positions will result in empowerment.

Although nine specific factors met the significance test, many of the factors were ones that the teachers already had worked on extensively. Therefore, a number of these factors failed the "uncertainty test." Specifically, the teachers felt quite certain about the following:

- Students feel that their opinions don't matter.
- Students feel that they are powerless.
- Students feel that schoolwork is busywork.
- Students see the purpose of schoolwork as getting credit.
- Students see schoolwork as largely irrelevant to their lives.
- Students need to share their work with decision makers.
- Students should advocate for positions.

This left just three issues or relationships that were both significant and that the researchers were still uncertain about:

- Will the students do their work on relevant social issues?
- Would the RWAPs they completed be of high enough quality to impress decision makers?
- Would advocacy and sharing lead to a greater sense of empowerment?

Applying the two-step test to their graphic reconstruction quickly reduced a complex and multifaceted issue to three specific action research questions that both Richard and Georgia deemed worthy of investigating.

The two-step test has two purposes:

- It makes the research process manageable in scope.
- It provides focuses for the inquiry.

Testing Your Focus—The Research Proposal

Some have said that conducting action research without a focus is akin to herding cats. A lack of focus is not only frustrating for action researchers; it often leads to abandonment of the inquiry altogether. After all, what dedicated teacher would spend time herding cats when the time could or should be spent investing in the planning and delivery of instruction?

The best way to ensure a sharp focus is to draft a written problem statement detailing precisely what is to be looked at and why. The problem statement is similar in many ways to the "research proposal" widely used in scholarly and professional communities. When scientists are seeking a grant to support a research project, they are required to submit a detailed written description of their plans. Graduate students who want approval from their advisor to conduct research for a master's thesis or a doctoral dissertation are also required to draft a detailed proposal providing answers to a specific set of questions, such as these:

- What do you want to study?
- Why is this issue of significance to you and the field?
- What specific aspects of this problem will you look at?
- What, if anything, have other researchers found out about this topic?
- What is your theoretical take on this topic?
- How will you collect the data needed to answer your questions?

Research proposals submitted to governmental and private foundations by scientists and dissertation proposals submitted by doctoral students often exceed a hundred pages. That is an undertaking that few rational teachers would ever volunteer to complete! However, you needn't despair. Although it is important to answer many of the same questions, we have learned that a mere page or two will suffice quite nicely for action research purposes. In fact, at Project LEARN we stated: "If an action research proposal runs more than two pages, it is probably too long and reflects a lack of focus. Therefore, you need to think more because you are not ready to proceed."

Implementation Strategy #6— *The Research Proposal/Problem Statement*

WHAT:
A process for ensuring focus for collaborative inquiry and/or explaining to colleagues what, specifically, the researcher(s), will be pursuing

HOW:
Draft concise answers to the following questions:

1. Who is affected by the problem? (Which students or which categories of students and teachers are affected by this issue?)

2. What is the nature of the problem? (Is this an issue of skills, attitudes, knowledge, or something else?)

3. What is suspected of causing the problem? (What do you believe has brought this about and is contributing to its continuation as a problem?)

4. What, if anything, do you intend to do to address this problem? (Is there an intervention or interventions that you already have in mind?)

5. What is the goal for improvement? (How would you like to see things turn out?)

6. What do you need or want to know about this problem? (What are your specific action research questions?)

7. How will you go about getting the data to answer your research questions? (This question will be addressed in the next chapter.)

To appreciate just how concise a focused problem statement can be, let's look at the problem statement/research proposal that Richard and Georgia drafted using the steps outlined in Implementation Strategy #6:

Social Efficacy Problem Statement/RWAP Research Proposal

Many of our 8th grade civics students hold feelings of powerlessness and a defeatist attitude that results in low levels of social efficacy.

We believe that the root of this problem is a lack of knowledge and skill in attacking complex social issues, coupled with a lack of experience in social advocacy.

Because we want all of our students to become socially efficacious, we intend to engage each of them in the development and execution of a Real World Advocacy Project (RWAP).

To determine the effectiveness of this approach in building social efficacy, we will need/want to know the following:

1. Can we motivate our students to complete RWAPs?
2. Will the RWAPs that the students complete be of high quality?
3. Will completion of a RWAP project lead to greater social efficacy for our students?

Although Richard and Georgia's proposal may not yet be complete, they are, nevertheless, able to share it with peers, colleagues, and supervisors as a statement of an issue they are concerned about to the extent that they are willing to devote professional energy toward developing deeper understanding. The last element of a research proposal, the plan for data collection, is the topic of the next chapter.

7 Data Collection: Using Teacher Records and Observation Data

Once you have found a focus for action research, clarified your theories regarding that focus, and identified research questions that are worth answering, it is time to begin the search for data. The next three chapters should provide the guidance you need to find adequate answers to your research questions.

A good place to start looking for data is where data already exist. Only when existing data or artifacts are unavailable or inadequate is it necessary to create new instruments. (Chapter 8 discusses the construction of new data collection instruments.)

Think of data as artifacts or evidence left behind by the phenomenon you are investigating. Educators spend their entire working lives in data-rich environments. Whenever school is open, data are produced. Often the information is on what the students have accomplished. This evidence appears in their portfolios or on the walls of their classrooms. Likewise, what the students *haven't* done generates data. Data on those disappointing nonevents can be found in teacher grade books, on student transcripts, and in copies of the notes sent home to parents.

This chapter deals with several types of data that are readily available in the form of teacher records and observations of the daily classroom experience.

Teacher Records

Various kinds of teacher records are valuable as sources of data. Among the most useful are lesson plans and grade books.

Lesson Plans

The lesson plans that most teachers use are a great source of action research data for several reasons. First, they contain a compilation of instructional activities arranged in chronological order. It is often helpful to convert these data into a time line (not unlike the time lines students might produce to demonstrate their knowledge of history). If Georgia and Richard (the teachers we met in Chapter 6) drew a time line for their RWAP project, it might look like the one illustrated in Figure 7.1.

FIGURE 7.1

Real World Advocacy Project: Teaching Time Line

Introduce assignment	February 1
Students choose topics/groups	February 10
Groups submit tentative work plan	February 28
Work on summaries of research	March 1–30
First draft of research summaries due	March 31
Work on action plans	April 1–14
First draft of action plans due	April 14
Development of presentations	April 15–May 1
Role play of presentations for class	May 1–15
Presentations to decision makers	May 15–June 1

Implementation Strategy #7—Creating an Instructional Time Line

WHAT:

An accurate report on what was taught, and when and how it was taught

MATERIALS:

Large piece of poster board or poster paper

HOW:

1. Draw a line across the bottom of the paper. Divide the line into time periods—weeks or days spent on content being studied.

2. Review the section of your plan book that covers the instruction provided to students during the period of the study. Above the divided line at the bottom of the paper, indicate the pertinent classroom assignments and events that relate to the issue being studied. If classroom activities took more than one day, indicate all of the time spent on the activity.

3. Review your time line to determine if it provides an accurate depiction of the work you engaged in when facilitating the students' learning of this material.

Teacher Grade Books

As an action researcher, you can easily conduct trend analyses by placing student performance data from your grade book onto your time line. This kind of trend data often proves quite helpful because it allows you determine if an individual student's performance is, or was, improving, declining, or remaining stable. Similarly, plotting the trend of an entire class or an entire school will illustrate whether the changes were positive, negative, or nonexistent. Furthermore, when you disaggregate the data by gender, ethnicity, and other factors, you can clearly observe how different subpopulations are faring in your classroom or in your school.

Although information on student performance is interesting, by itself it doesn't indicate how to improve teaching. However, when trends in student performance are correlated with classroom plans, it's possible to learn a great deal about the effectiveness of each chosen strategy.

Functionally, what is being suggested here is a form of historical analysis. A good illustration of this is the finding that lowering highway speed limits results in fewer traffic fatalities. This commonly accepted fact was established by precisely this type of trend analysis. For years the National Traffic Safety Board gathered statistics on the rate of highway fatalities in the United States. For years those rates stayed relatively stable. Then a strange thing happened. Transportation researchers noticed that the rate of deaths per thousand passenger miles dropped dramatically during the summer of 1973. The researchers wondered why this had happened. What was it about the summer of 1973 that made driving safer?

Before answering that question, let's consider an analogous trend analysis involving the math performance of a 3rd grade student, Jose. Jose's teacher recorded his weekly grades on homework and quizzes in her grade book. She noticed that his schoolwork was in no way exceptional during the first four months of the school year. However, beginning in January both his grades and behavior took a remarkable jump.

Both of these findings—the drop in highway fatalities in 1973 and the improvement in Jose's performance during the second semester—should be cause for celebration. But beyond celebrating, what might we learn from these occurrences that would help us in the future?

The process that historians use to answer that question is to place all the relevant historical information onto a time line and then search for correlates. When researchers did this with the traffic fatality data, a powerful insight surfaced. In July 1973, in response to a drastic fuel shortage resulting from an oil embargo, the speed limit on all U.S. highways was reduced to 55 miles per hour as a conservation measure. The drop in highway fatalities corresponds almost exactly to the date of that policy change. Although direct cause and effect relationships may be impossible to prove in situations such as this, the correlation between the change in speed limit and the rate of automobile fatalities has led most safety experts to conclude that speed limit policy is a significant factor in reducing the highway death rate.

In Jose's case, his teacher might build a time line by using the information from her lesson plans and annotating it with data from an interview she conducted with Jose. The interview revealed that Jose received a computer and math software as a Christmas present from his grandparents. Furthermore, the lesson plans showed that during the second semester, much of the assigned homework was of a type that could be completed with the use of a computer. Later, an examination of Jose's portfolio would indicate that, in fact, he had done most of his second-semester work on his new computer. Based upon these data, the teacher could surmise that the availability of a computer at home, coupled with the kind of homework assigned during second semester, contributed to Jose's remarkable improvement.

Implementation Strategy #8—Conducting a Trend Analysis

WHAT:
A process to help identify instructional factors that significantly influence student performance

MATERIALS:
Your instructional time line (Implementation Strategy #7), and your grade book

HOW:
1. Look for indicators of behavior and performance (for example, attendance, office referrals, homework completion, quizzes, etc.) for the student(s) whose work you intend to study.

2. For each of the indicators identified above, list on a separate sheet of paper the student's score or the average score for the group of students being studied and the date achieved.

3. Plot this information on your time line or on a separate transparent sheet that can be placed directly on top of your time line.

4. Look for significant changes in student performance and then examine what occurred in the classroom at the time these changes were observed. List the observed changes and the events that coincided with them.

5. Generate a list of concise narrative statements regarding any observed changes in student performance and the corresponding classroom events.

Observational Data

Classroom observations provide another rich and readily available source of data. Such observations can be made and recorded by teachers themselves or by outside observers. A number of recording tools simplify this form of data collection.

Journals

Student behavior is data. Furthermore, it occurs all the time, right in front of you. The problem is that, unless you deliberately capture these data in a timely fashion, they are likely to fade from your memory.

If you establish the habit of keeping a journal, you will create a treasure trove of data. I know many teachers who have developed brilliant action research projects drawing data exclusively from their journal entries. A trend analysis of journal data can help you retrospectively understand why things transpired in a particular fashion and followed a particular sequence. If you've never developed the journal habit and aren't motivated to begin, there are a number of other ways to capture observational data about classroom events as they occur.

Clipboard Notes

Get a clipboard and keep it in a permanent place on your desk, never out of reach. Whenever you witness an event that may be relevant to the topic you are researching, jot it down. Even the briefest of notes can awaken memories later (when you're doing data analysis). In addition, the very things you jot down are often pieces of data themselves. For example, comments regarding the students' reaction to a lesson you were teaching or the work they were engaged in are important pieces of data concerning your instructional work. Finally, an event in the classroom can raise new questions you might wish to consider, and your clipboard then becomes your action research to-do list of things you will want to follow up on.

When taking notes using the clipboard method, it's important to date everything you jot down. Although it may be months before you look at your notes, if they include a date and time, they will be a valuable asset for a trend analysis.

Open-Ended Checklists

Sometimes you need detailed observational data that you can't obtain yourself. This is often the case when you want to observe what is happening while you are teaching. Unless you have eyes in the back of your head, this presents numerous challenges. A good solution is to use the services of a colleague who is able and willing to spend an instructional period observing in your classroom. Observational data are usually taken and shared in the form of a checklist. Most types of observational data for action research purposes involve one of two types of checklists: *open-ended* or *predefined*.

Figures 7.2 and 7.3 (p. 85) are examples of open-ended checklists. Both of these lists were developed to produce a concise (single-page) picture of the instructional activities occurring one day across 70 different classrooms in a comprehensive high school. In this case the observer/data collector went into each classroom with a blank sheet of paper. The data collector's mission was to capture the full array and distribution of teachers' instructional activities and students' classroom experiences on a typical school day. The data collector accomplished this by recording a "snapshot" of data every 30 seconds during 70 separate five-minute classroom visits. As classroom activities unfolded, the data

FIGURE 7.2

Open-Ended Checklist of Observed Teacher Activities
(632 Snapshots of Teacher Activities)

Activity	No. of snapshots where observed	Percentage of total snapshots*
Responding to or helping individual students	112	18%
Asking questions	100	16%
Lecturing	91	14%
Paperwork (at desk)	42	7%
Active monitoring (looking for students needing help)	41	6%
Getting materials	38	6%
Administering tests (proctoring)	27	4%
Management (attendance, organizational details)	27	4%
Audiovisual equipment set-up	25	4%
Observing student performance	23	4%
Responding to student questions	20	3%
Absent from room	16	3%
Giving directions on an assignment	12	2%
Demonstrating for students	11	2%
Cleaning up after lab	9	1%
Small-group instruction	8	1%
Correcting homework	5	1%
Listening to recitations	5	1%

FIGURE 7.2—*continued*

Open-Ended Checklist of Observed Teacher Activities
(632 Snapshots of Teacher Activities)

Activity	No. of snapshots where observed	Percentage of total snapshots*
Miscellaneous	5	1%
Admonishing student(s)	5	1%
Waiting for attention	2	.3%
Monitoring student behavior	2	.3%
Calling on a student	2	.3%
Discussion	2	.3%
Dealing with interruptions	1	.2%
Social interaction with students	1	.2%

*Due to rounding off, these percentages do not add up to 100.

—Adapted from *How to Conduct Collaborative Action Research*, p. 36 (Sagor, 1993).

collector noted them on a list of continually expanding categories. Whenever a new category of student or teacher behavior was observed, the data collector added it to the list; if a previously observed behavior was observed a second or third time, the data collector simply noted it with another slash mark.

When using an open-ended checklist, the data collector need not be concerned that the list of categories is becoming too long. Categories can always be combined with like categories at the conclusion of the data collection process.

Predefined Checklists

When you know precisely what you are looking for before starting the observation process, you can use a predefined checklist. One difference between the predefined and the open-ended checklist is that the predefined checklist requires that you (and your action research colleagues, if this is a team effort) spend time defining "observation criteria" before commencing data collection. Figure 7.4 (p. 86) is an example of a predefined checklist. This is a time-on-task chart focusing on three students in a 3rd grade classroom.

Data obtained through predefined checklists can be quite helpful, provided that all the data collectors, as well as those receiving the data, fully agree on the definitions and criteria being employed to classify each action. This is especially true when using multiple data collectors. It is clear agreement on criteria that guarantees what researchers call *inter-rater reliability*. The development of precise definitions or criteria emerges as the by-product of unhurried professional discussion. If you elect to use this approach, you must be willing to devote considerable time and energy to refining observational criteria before you begin data collection. The definitions that emerge must be both unambiguous and observable. For example, the definitions used for the time-on-task data collection reported in Figure 7.4 were as follows:

On Task: Whenever the student is engaging in behavior either directly requested by the teacher or clearly inferred from the assigned activity

Off Task: Whenever the student is engaging in behavior that is other than that requested by the teacher or is incompatible with the behavior requested by the teacher

Using those definitions, if an observer noticed a student discussing a math concept with a classmate during a cooperative learning activity, they would mark it as "on task." Similarly, another student seen quietly listening to his teacher while she delivered a lecture would have that behavior marked as "on task." Conversely, a data collector following the above definitions would classify a student as "off task" if the student was observed talking to a classmate during a lecture or reading a library book during a cooperative learning exercise.

Figure 7.5 (p. 88) shows data drawn from another type of predefined checklist. This list is an aggregation of data on the cognitive level of instructional activities on a particular day at a comprehensive high school. Before collecting these data, members of the action research team worked together to achieve consensus on definitions as to what constituted an activity appropriate for each identified cognitive level: comprehension, application, analysis, synthesis, and evaluation.

It's important to realize that even definitions that appear straightforward can be subject to a certain degree of interpretation. One way to

FIGURE 7.3

Open-Ended Checklist of Observed Student Activities
(643 Snapshots of Student Activities)

Activity	No. of snapshots where observed	Percentage of total snapshots*
Seatwork	142	22%
Listening to teacher	112	17%
Responding to questions from teacher	91	14%
Lab work	88	14% *
Taking tests	65	10%
Visiting with one another	25	4%
Performing	18	3%
Reciting	14	2%
Asking the teacher questions	14	2%
Watching or listening to audio-visual materials	13	2%
Getting out materials	12	2%
Group work	10	2%
Cleaning up	10	2%
Observing performance	8	1%
Discussion	8	1%
Responding to questions in writing	5	.8%
Responding to management questions	4	.6%
Observing teacher demonstrations	2	.3%
Waiting	2	.3%

*Due to rounding off, these percentages do not add up to 100.

—Adapted from Sagor (1993, p. 37).

FIGURE 7.4

Predefined Checklist
Two-Minute Interval Time-on-Task Record

✔ = on   0 = off

Activity	Jayne	Jason	Jennifer
Instructions	✔	✔	✔
	✔	✔	✔
Group Work	✔	✔	✔
	O	✔	✔
	O	✔	✔
	✔	O	✔
	✔	✔	✔
	✔	✔	✔
	O	✔	✔
Cleanup	O	✔	✔
	O	✔	✔
Video	✔	O	✔
	✔	✔	✔
	✔	O	✔
	✔	✔	✔
	✔	✔	✔

FIGURE 7.4—*continued*

Predefined Checklist
Two-Minute Interval Time-on-Task Record

✔ = on   O = off

Activity	Jayne	Jason	Jennifer
Desk Work	✔	✔	✔
	O	✔	✔
	O	✔	✔
	O	✔	✔
	✔	O	✔
	✔	O	✔
Classroom Discussion	✔	✔	✔
	✔	✔	✔
	O	✔	✔
	O	O	✔
	✔	✔	✔
	63%	78%	100%

know that your definitions are sufficiently precise is to see if several teachers (members of your action research team) can independently observe the same classroom episode and rate the behavior of individual students identically. You can do this by using videotaped classroom vignettes. When several teachers watch the same tape and classify the behavior similarly, they have achieved inter-rater reliability.

Each of the examples of a predefined checklist discussed so far involves a straightforward decision—whether an identified behavior or

FIGURE 7.5

Predefined Checklist
Cognitive Level of Lessons in a High School

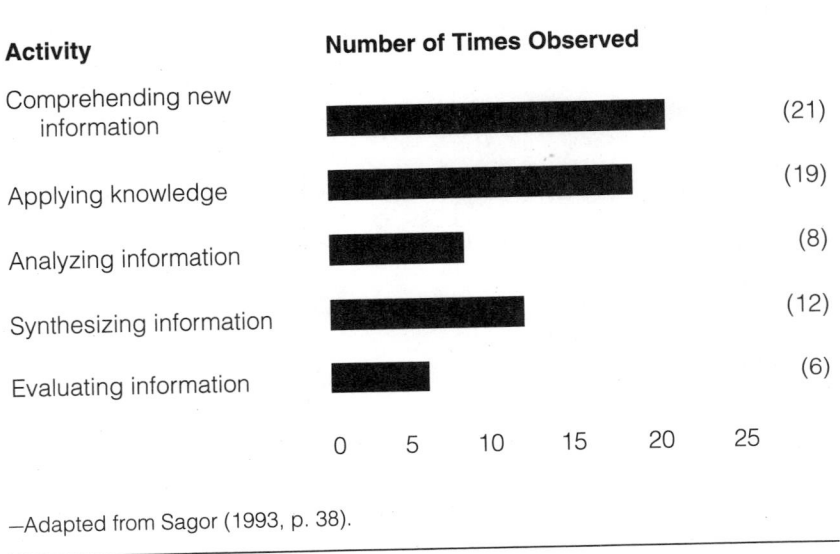

Activity   **Number of Times Observed**

Comprehending new   (21)
  information

Applying knowledge   (19)

Analyzing information   (8)

Synthesizing information   (12)

Evaluating information   (6)

          0   5   10   15   20   25

—Adapted from Sagor (1993, p. 38).

phenomenon is present or absent. We might call these "either/or" checklists. Although either/or checklists work well for issues like "time on task" or the "cognitive level" of lessons, they aren't the only kind of predefined checklists you might wish to employ. Sometimes your research question calls for a different type of checklist—for example, one that necessitates assessing a behavior against a predetermined continuum of performance. When you need this kind of tool, you can turn to another type of predefined checklist, the rating scale or scoring guide, more commonly called the *rubric*. (See Chapter 6 for information on the development of rubrics.)

Rating Scales

An example from outside the field of education illustrates the value of this type of comparative assessment. Consider the job of an Olympic diving judge. Putting aside political considerations and possible favoritism, the closeness among different judges' assessments is impressive. It is not surprising to see 10 judges (each using a 10-point scale) all scoring a particular dive within four-tenths of a point of each other. How are they able to do this when the dive took only two seconds? The way that judges achieve such high levels of inter-rater reliability is by first becoming extremely clear about two things: (1) traits they intend to evaluate and (2) criteria they will use for evaluating each trait. These factors are then incorporated into a scoring guide.

For example, when judging divers, the officials might agree to assess four elements: the take-off, the mid-air flight, the entry, and the degree of difficulty. They also have to decide if each element should receive equal weight in the scoring system. Assume that the judges agree to equal weight for each element, with a maximum score of 2.5 if the element is performed perfectly and a score of zero if the element is performed incompetently. They then need to create a developmental continuum for each of these four "essential" elements. For example, for entry they might determine that a perfect score of 2.5 would be granted whenever a diver entered the water (1) at a perfect 90-degree angle and (2) with almost no splash. In contrast, a belly flop would garner a score of zero. The judges then need to define what a mid-range entry would look like—one that might earn a score of 1.25. When all the criteria have been delineated, a scoring continuum has been established. Still, the judges need to test the clarity of these expectations. They could do this by having multiple judges score the same videotaped dive in an effort to create high consistency (inter-rater reliability) in scoring.

Now let's apply this to classroom research. Many teachers have adopted a 5-point scale to use with their scoring rubrics. In Project LEARN, we decided that our rubrics should imply a never-ending continuum of competence. Furthermore, we wanted them to provide motivation for our students. For these reasons, on our 5-point rating scales a score of 1 meant basic competence (a totally incompetent student would not be scored), and a score of 5 indicated fluent performance (the word *fluent* leaves the door open for further growth).

We created our rubrics by first asking the question:

Where would we be likely to find most of our competent students after a successful instructional experience?

Then we specified the observable behaviors or products we would expect to see from these students and agreed to give such observable behaviors and products a score of 3. Next we asked:

What type of performance would we likely see from a student whose work was truly exceptional?

We assigned such work a score of 5. Next we asked:

What type of work would we likely get from a student whose performance was only minimally acceptable?

Such work (what we would expect to receive from a novice student) was assigned a performance rating of 1. Our final step was filling in the scale with the behavior or attributes we expected to see in a 2.0 or a 4.0 performance.

In Chapter 6 you met Georgia and Richard, the 8th grade social studies teachers who wanted to improve the social efficacy of their students through the introduction of a Real World Advocacy Project (RWAP). You saw the rubric their colleagues developed to determine the impact on their dependent variable, social efficacy. Although the rubric would prove helpful for these teachers, it wasn't the only measuring device they would need.

You may recall that after they applied the "two-step test" to their graphic reconstruction, three important research questions emerged:

• Could we motivate our 8th graders to conduct and complete Real World Advocacy Projects?
• What would be the quality of the projects produced by our students?
• Would the completion of Real World Advocacy Projects result in enhanced feelings of social efficacy for our students?

Each question focused the researchers on a different achievement target, which had to be assessed. The target in the first question, *conducting and completing a collaborative project,* calls for an either/or assessment. After all a student's project is either completed or it isn't. However, the targets involved in the second and third questions, *the quality of the projects produced* and the development of *feelings of social efficacy,* call for assessments using a rating scale.

The rubric developed to measure social efficacy (Figure 6.1, p. 64) proved helpful in answering the third question. But Richard and Georgia needed an additional tool. Specifically, they had to decide what criteria to use to assess the completed RWAP projects. They felt this was essential if they were to adequately answer the second research question.

At first they considered simply assigning letter grades, but they rejected this idea as being far too subjective. Instead they decided to create a 4-trait scoring guide (using the Project LEARN guidelines discussed above) that independent evaluators could use to reliably score the final projects. Doing this required the teachers to follow two sequential steps:

Step 1: Decide what were the critical aspects (traits) of the RWAPs that should be judged.

Step 2: Determine the range of proficiencies they wanted to assess.

It should be obvious by now that developing a rating scale is a time-consuming process. It takes time because if it is to be a truly helpful assessment tool, it must be written in unambiguous language. It must clearly differentiate between performances that receive different scores, and it must control for extraneous or intervening variables. (This topic will be discussed further in Chapter 9).

Ultimately, Georgia and Richard devised a scoring guide that was satisfactory to both of them. Figure 7.6 (pp. 93–94) shows the scoring guide that emerged from their collaborative work.

....

Implementation Strategy #9—Developing a Rating Scale for Assessing Student Work

WHAT:
Setting criteria to assess the quality of student work

HOW:
1. Discuss with a partner the traits that are important components of the work you want your students to produce. List these traits.

2. For each trait, discuss specific observable behaviors or performances that you expect to see from *competent* students. Make sure these descriptors are discrete, unambiguous, and easily understood. Assign these behaviors or products a score of 3.

3. Discuss and agree on the *minimum* descriptor, behavior, or performance you would accept as a demonstration of this skill. Select descriptors for this performance that are discrete, unambiguous, and easily understood. Assign these behaviors or products a score of 1.

4. Discuss and agree on the behavior or performance that you would consider an *exemplary* demonstration of this skill. Select descriptors for this

performance that are discrete, unambiguous, and easily understood. Assign these behaviors or products a score of 5.

5. Discuss and agree on behaviors or performances you might observe that fall incrementally between the scores you've already identified. Select descriptors for these performances that are discrete, unambiguous, and easily understood. Assign these behaviors and products a score of 2 and 4.

6. Share and discuss the rating scale with one or more colleagues seeking to achieve consensus on an understanding of the targets and the scoring criteria.

7. After reaching agreement, pat yourself on the back. You have just produced a rating scale that will help you measure the success of your efforts on the dependent variable.

. . . .

The techniques discussed in this chapter should help you document what is going on in your classroom. The next chapter presents additional observation techniques and then goes on to examine the development of instruments that can assist in probing what is happening below the surface. Specifically, it discusses the survey and interview as techniques to find out what people really know, what they are thinking, and how they are feeling.

FIGURE 7.6

Scoring Guide for the Real World Advocacy Project

TRAIT	EMERGING 1	BASIC 2	DEVELOPING 3	COMPETENT 4	FLUENT 5
Plan of action	Lists actions that could be taken.	Lists actions to be taken in a logical order.	Lists actions in logical and priority order, specifying person(s) responsible.	Lists and discusses actions explaining priorities, time lines, and responsibilities.	Provides alternative plans, each organized in priority order with time lines and responsibilities. Pros and cons of alternative plans are addressed.
Evidence of personal growth	Reports on specific things learned from the project.	Reports specific learnings from the project and refers to how learned.	Reports learnings from project, describes how learning was acquired, providing possible academic applications.	Reports learnings from the project, demonstrates an understanding of how the learning was accomplished, and generalizes learning to other circumstances.	Provides evidence of changes in personal problem solving as a result of the experience. Shows evidence of integrating the learning in academic and personal matters.

FIGURE 7.6—continued

Scoring Guide for the Real World Advocacy Project

TRAIT	EMERGING 1	BASIC 2	DEVELOPING 3	COMPETENT 4	FLUENT 5
Organization and thoughtfulness of plan	Restates the problem and a desire for change.	There is a plan, but only minimal consideration is given to long-range impact.	Proposes a generally clear and reasonable plan. Long-range impacts are apparent.	Proposes a clear and viable plan with specific recommendations. Long-range impacts are considered and dealt with appropriately.	Proposes a thoughtful plan addressing reasonably anticipated objections. Recommendations focus on minimizing negative impacts and maximizing long-range benefits.
Provision of reasoned alternative solutions	Offers minimal suggestions for solutions.	Suggests specific solutions.	Suggests specific solutions backed by evidence.	Suggests a range of solutions backed by evidence.	Suggests a continuum of solutions weighed by evidence of their appropriateness and effectiveness.

8 Data Collection: Creating Instruments to Answer Research Questions

Chapter 7 reviewed strategies to collect data that already exist or that a trained observer could easily collect. Although the data collection techniques covered in this chapter require that you develop some new instrumentation, they offer significant potential benefits in helping you understand what is happening in your classroom and in your school.

Shadowing

One popular and powerful way to collect observational data in educational settings is through *shadowing* (Sagor, 1981). You can use shadowing when you want to see a phenomenon from the perspective of someone else. When shadowing, you figuratively put yourself in another person's shoes and attempt to experience an event as though you were that person. The most common type of shadowing done by teacher researchers is the observation of a particular student or set of students. Typically this is done by freeing the teacher from regular duties and allowing the teacher to follow the schedule of a student whose school experience the teacher wishes to understand better.

You can use any of the three types of checklists discussed in Chapter 7 (open-ended checklist, predefined checklist, or rating scale) when you shadow. Figure 8.1 (p. 97) is a predefined checklist that a group of high school teachers used when they shadowed students to gain a better understanding of the degree to which their students experienced effective schooling practices. Figure 8.2 (p. 98) is an observational checklist used by an elementary school faculty that wanted to learn more about how their school climate was experienced by three categories of students (the average achiever, the above-average student, and the underachiever).

As a result of our experience in Project LEARN, my colleagues and I have developed two sets of guidelines to facilitate a positive shadowing experience. We have found that the shadowing process differs by grade level and school organization patterns. For this reason, we have created separate guidelines for elementary (self-contained) classrooms and secondary schools.

Shadowing Guidelines for Elementary (Self-Contained) Classrooms

Number of students. You should be able to successfully shadow up to three students in the same self-contained classroom.

Selection of students. If your project will require disaggregation of data, you should plan to observe a cross section of the student body that includes each demographic category your research will explore—for example, high-, middle-, and low-achieving students. The person doing the shadowing asks the teacher in whose room the shadowing is to occur to identify students who are typical of each of these categories. If other teachers are shadowing in your room, it is your job to provide them with this information.

Anonymity. As a rule, you don't need to inform the children being observed that they are being watched until after the shadowing has occurred.

Time frame. Shadowing for a half day (generally the morning), when the basic skills are taught, usually provides enough insight on the child's school experience.

Dates for shadowing. Although no two days are ever typical, it is wise to avoid days that are unique (days before holidays, testing days, etc.).

Debriefing with students. For purposes of triangulation, you should end the shadowing approximately one-half hour before you must leave for your other commitments. Use that time to interview the children you have observed. Explore with the kids the same issues that were on the observation checklist. You may begin your interview with a comment such as this:

> When I was in your class today, I couldn't help but observe you working. Would you mind if I asked you some questions about your work this morning?

FIGURE 8.1

Shadowing Checklist for Determining the Presence of Effective Schooling Practices at a High School

Taking this school day as a whole, do you feel the student would have:	YES	NO	Undecided or no response
1. Felt the school had high expectations for his/her achievement?	2	5	1
2. Felt the climate in the school was orderly and conducive to learning?	5	2	1
3. Felt the instruction provided was based on data regarding his/her understanding?	4	2	2
4. Felt the instructional materials made available were appropriate to help him/her learn?	5	3	0
5. Felt his/her good school work and effort were appreciated?	5	3	0
6. Felt his/her day was structured to provide the maximum opportunity to learn? (Academic learning time)	2	6	0
7. Felt most of his/her class time was spent productively and on task?	2	5	1
8. Felt the school was dedicated primarily to the process of learning?	3	3	2
9. Felt he/she was an active participant in the teaching/learning process?	3	3	2

—Adapted from Sagor, R. D. (1981, December). A day in the life: A technique for assessing school climate and effectiveness. *Educational Leadership, 39*(2), 190–193.

FIGURE 8.2

Shadowing Checklist for an Elementary School

School Climate Questions	Above-Average Performer	Average Performer	Below-Average Performer
Taking this day as a whole, would the child have:	Yes/No Why?	Yes/No Why?	Yes/No Why?
1. Felt the school had high expectations for his or her achievement?			
2. Felt the climate in the school was orderly and conducive to learning?			
3. Felt the instruction provided was based on data regarding his or her understanding? (Monitoring)			
4. Felt the instructional materials made available were appropriate to help him or her learn?			
5. Felt his or her good school work and effort were appreciated?			
6. Felt his or her day was structured to provide the maximum opportunity to learn? (Academic learning time)			
7. Felt most of his or her class time was spent productively and on task?			
8. Felt the school was dedicated primarily to the process of learning?			
9. Felt he or she was an active participant in the teaching/learning process?			
10. Felt competent?			
11. Felt a sense of belonging?			
12. Felt useful?			
13. Felt potent?			
14. Felt optimistic?			

If the student agrees, you can then proceed to paraphrase each question from the observation checklist in kid-friendly language. For example, if the checklist asks for data on "time on task," you might ask the following:

> I was watching you after Ms. Smith gave the class instructions. Were you doing what she expected the students to be doing at reading time this morning?

Shadowing Guidelines for Secondary School

Number of students. Plan to shadow one student at a time.

Selection of students. If the goal is to understand how a cross section of students experiences the school, then you will need to draw a stratified random sample of students. You can do this by dividing a school roster into categories that represent each demographic group of interest—for example, gender, past academic achievement, ethnicity, age.

Anonymity. You should not only tell secondary students in advance that they will be shadowed, but you should ask the students' permission. This shouldn't be a concern. In fact, most students are flattered that we care enough to spend the time learning about their school experience.

Time frame. You should plan to shadow for an entire school day or a series of days that together represent the student's full school experience.

Dates for shadowing. Although no two days are ever typical, it is wise to avoid days that are unique (days before holidays, testing days, etc.).

Debriefing with students. If multiple teachers are shadowing at the same school, you should schedule a debriefing meeting attended by all the teachers and students involved in the shadowing to compare and contrast their experiences. A record of this meeting can provide helpful data to use for triangulation.

Teacher Notes and Comments

Just as the events that occur in your room are data, so is everything that you or your students produce. A handy tool for keeping copies of notes is carbonless paper. If you write comments to students on their work, consider writing them on carbonless paper. This gives both you and the student a record of what you have said. Looking back at all the comments that you have made to a student over the course of the term enables you to observe trends. The data may show whether the same mistakes were repeated, whether the student heeded your advice, and whether your comments tended to be positive or negative.

You can also use carbonless paper to keep track of notes sent home to parents or to counselors regarding particular students. Often these notes contain valuable insights that might get lost in the myriad of things happening in a busy teacher's life. Verbatim copies tend to bring it all back, sometimes all too vividly!

Student Work

To analyze data on students' achievement, nothing is more valid than the work they produce. When work that is taken home is thrown into a wastebasket, all that's left are faint traces of the real work—marks in the grade book. An actual student paper will always contain far more robust data regarding writing competence then any possible grade. There are many excellent instructional reasons to have students keep their work in portfolios. However, even if portfolios are not a part of your current classroom routine, you can still find ways to keep your students' work without having to sacrifice communication with parents.

I do this by establishing a classroom policy that states that students must take all work home, share it with parents, and then return it (initialed by the parent or guardian) within two days. Later I store each student's work in a separate folder. When the year is over, if I don't need the work as action research data, I either return it to the student or give it a dignified burial in the circular file. If, however, I want to take a retrospective look at the growth of any individual student or the class as a whole, my folders of goodies will be the most authentic and valid evidence I could ever obtain.

Reflections on Checklist, Rating Scale, or Portfolio Data

Records of discussions or collections of written comments are other sources of valuable data for action research. In the case discussed in Chapter 7 of the high school studying the use of class time, after spending a few hours thoroughly reviewing their data (Figures 7.2 and 7.3, pp. 82–83, 85), the faculty discussed the five questions shown in Figure 8.3.

The data from the discussion provided focus for school improvement efforts at that high school for the next two years.

FIGURE 8.3.

Reflection Questions

1. What are the implications of the findings that teachers spend a high percentage of their time questioning, but a small percentage of time actually engaging students in class discussions?

2. Should the percentage of time spent on small-group instruction be a cause for concern?

3. What does the individual student experience when his/her teacher is using a large-group lecture/questioning strategy?

4. What is the impact on the total class when the teacher is spending time helping individual students?

5. What percentage of the student day do you think should be spent on

____ (a) Listening?
____ (b) Writing, computing, working in their seats?
____ (c) Reciting, performing, discussing?
____ (d) Lab work, hands-on activities?
____ (e) Off-task?
____ (f) Other:

Another example of using reflection as a source of data comes from the experience of teachers who regularly use student portfolios for assessment. When rating scales or rubrics are well developed and used properly, students can effectively use them to assess their own work. Students who assess what they produce can then provide their teachers (as well as themselves) valuable data regarding their perceptions of their work, their learning, and their future plans. Figure 8.4 shows a generic prompt I have used to assist students in reflecting on their completed work.

I ask students to fill out the answers to these questions on a one-page worksheet, which I then have them attach to the piece of work. The work as well as the reflections ultimately reside in the student portfolio. With younger or nonliterate children, an aide or parent volunteer can collect these same types of reflections using audiotapes. A third strategy for collecting student perceptions is to hold a classroom discussion, which can be audiotaped. Whichever technique is used, students' own reflections on their work provide a rich source of data for any action researcher who is interested in monitoring and understanding student performance.

Student Journals

Just as teacher journals can be a valuable source of data, so too can student journals. Frequently teachers have students keep a journal as a regular aspect of instruction. It is not uncommon to have students regularly keep math journals, reading journals, and even open-ended journals containing their reflections on their own learning. These are not only a wonderful source of data, but when it comes to reporting (discussed in Chapter 11), student quotes add immeasurable depth to research conclusions.

FIGURE 8.4

Reflection Questions for Students' Portfolio Products

1. What feature of this work pleased you most?

2. What aspect of this work would you change?

3. What new learning or skill was demonstrated by this piece of work?

4. Based upon what you learned with this piece of work, what will you do differently on your next project?

Note: If you plan on using student work in public reports of your research, it is only ethical and appropriate to secure the student's permission in advance, even when you make efforts to mask the student's identity. (Chapter 12 discusses this and additional ethical considerations.)

If student journals are not a regular aspect of your classroom, you can still use this technique episodically. When attempting to collect data on a classroom project—during an innovative three-week unit, for example—you can stop class a few minutes early and ask the students to respond on index cards to a prompt such as one of the following:

- What did you find most useful in today's lesson? Why?
- What did you find most frustrating in today's lesson? Why?
- Would you like to do this sort of work again? Why?

If that doesn't sound significant, consider this: If you do this with just one class of 30 students, by the end of three weeks you will have collected 450 separate student reflections on a pertinent aspect of your teaching!

Logs

An even simpler way to collect data on student involvement is to use a log. A log is a document in which participants are required to record information on what they are doing and when. For example, you could use a computer log if you wanted to gather information about technology usage in your school or classroom. Every morning for a month, you could tape a log sheet, like the one shown in Figure 8.5 (p. 105), next to each computer in your classroom. You could then instruct students to note the time they logged on to the computer, their name, the software they used, and what purpose they used it for (an assignment, research, games, e-mail, etc.)

Doing this for even a month wouldn't require much of your time. But by the end of the month, you would have data to answer all of these and other pertinent questions:

- Which students used the computer the most?
- Which students used computers the least?
- Was there a difference in computer use between boys and girls?
- What was the most frequently given reason for use of computers—class work, games, research, or e-mail?
- Was there a relationship between computer usage and academic performance (grades)?

Probes

The methods discussed thus far all have one thing in common: they are methods for collecting data that already exist. These techniques are but a few of the ways to capture what is going on above the surface. However, often you need to find out what's going on under the surface or hidden from clear view. This is particularly the case when you want answers to questions about what someone *understands* (cognitive knowledge) or what someone *thinks* (their opinions) or what someone *feels* (affective data). To obtain this information, you need to probe under the surface to illuminate what you cannot see. The three main vehicles for surfacing this type of hidden information are tests, surveys, and interviews.

Tests

Although we all use tests to arrive at grades for students, we should never forget that their primary purpose is to check for understanding. Test results tell us what individual students know and don't know how to do. Aggregating the scores allows us to see which elements of our teaching were successful for most of the students and which elements were unsuccessful for some.

Because you already have experience and expertise as a test developer, further guidance on test development is not presented here. Just remember that as a teacher researcher you may well want to include tests as part of a triangulated data collection plan.

Written Surveys

Probably no one form of data collection is used more often by teacher researchers than the written survey. It's popular because it's efficient and versatile. In 10 minutes you can survey an entire classroom of students or a hundred people attending a meeting. Depending on how you frame the questions, you can use surveys to gather data concerning affective, cognitive, or attitudinal issues. For example, you might ask questions such as these:

- What is the structure of the student council? (cognitive)
- What is your opinion of the quality of our student government? (attitudinal)
- How do you feel about working in student government? (affective)

The Survey Development Guidelines presented on p. 106 can help you develop an effective survey.

FIGURE 8.5

Computer Log

Student's Name	Log-In Time	Log-Out Time	Software Used	Purpose

Survey Development Guidelines*

• **Strive for clarity.** Conduct a small field test to make sure participants understand your survey questions. Ask one or more volunteers to try out the survey and then ask them if anything was unclear or misleading.

• **Strive for brevity.** As a general rule, try to develop surveys that take no longer than 10 minutes to administer.

• **Provide an opportunity for participants to make additional comments.** This helps in two ways. The respondents always feel that they had a chance to tell you what was on their minds, and open-ended responses often provide great insights for analysis.

• **Consider confidentiality issues in advance.** If you are afraid that people will be less than honest if the survey asks for their names, consider keeping the survey anonymous. However, some researchers believe people will be more inclined to give thoughtful answers if their names are included.

• **Consider disaggregation issues in advance.** If, when you are analyzing your data, you will want to divide and compare responses by sub-groups—for example, boys vs. girls, 8th graders vs. 7th graders, 5th period vs. 8th period—request the relevant information at the top of the survey form.

• **Remember that your first goal is credibility.** To ensure that even a skeptical colleague will believe your results, you should avoid suggesting a desired response (this is like a lawyer asking a leading question). For example, instead of asking, "Is student government effective in teaching about democracy?" ask "What are the purpose(s) of student government?" or "How do we teach democracy in this school?"

• **Try to separate fact from opinion by asking follow-up questions.** Examples include "How do you know?" or "What led you to this opinion?"

• **When using numerical scales, ask for an explanation of responses.** For example:

How would you rate student involvement in this school?

Poor		Average		Exceptional
1	2	3	4	5

What would it take to make your rating a 5?

• **Decide whether to use an odd- or even-numbered scale.** When using numerical scales, consider whether you want a scale that forces people to respond either positively or negatively (an even-numbered scale) or a scale that allows people to respond neutrally (an odd-numbered scale).

*Adapted from Sagor (1993, p. 39).

Written surveys offer the advantage of providing a great deal of information quickly. The drawback, however, is that the responses tend to be shallow. The interview is just the opposite. Interviews are time consuming, but they provide in-depth information.

Interviews

Most people enjoy being interviewed. The time the researcher is investing tells them someone really cares about what they think; nevertheless, the respondents' time must be respected. For this reason, you should, if at all possible, avoid the necessity for follow-up interviews. An interview guide can help you keep the discussion on track by serving as a general road map to help you direct the discussion in a manner that should produce relevant information and insights. The Interview Guidelines presented below offer some basic points to consider when developing an interview guide.

Interview Guidelines

• **Limit the number of questions.** Usually 10 to 15 question areas are sufficient.

• **Make sure the interview guide is comprehensive.** Reread your research questions before writing the first draft of the guide and review the research questions again after writing the guide to be sure you have asked for all relevant information.

• **Follow up on all factual and/or opinion questions.** Probe for further information with requests for examples or explanations.

• **Decide how you will collect the interview data.** Audiotaping the interview frees you from the need to take notes and allows you to make the interviewee more comfortable with eye contact and interaction. It also gives you a verbatim account for later use in analysis.

• **Strive for clarity.** Practice your interview with a friend. Ask for feedback on whether questions were clear.

• **Estimate the time required.** An interview should last no longer than 45 minutes.

• **Avoid suggesting desired responses.** Leading questions, body language, or hints regarding desired responses can adversely affect the objectivity of the responses.

You may find it useful to enlist the help of others in conducting interviews for data collection. Teachers at Aloha High School in Beaverton, Oregon, found an innovative and productive way to involve their students as interviewers. To find out what motivated students to work hard at school, the teachers enlisted the help of the 500 students enrolled in senior English. They taught them the skills of interviewing, and then these senior students, working in pairs, interviewed three other students using the same protocol. Each pair of student interviewers wrote summaries of the data they collected. The teacher researchers then reviewed the resulting 250 summaries, which contained the reflections of 750 students. Using this process, these teacher researchers gathered a huge amount of information without needing to conduct the interviews themselves (Henstrand and Johnson, 1993).

This strategy provided numerous benefits beyond simply saving the teacher researchers time. The student interviewers were graded on their work; probably because the work was "authentic" and appeared meaningful for the students, the completion rate and quality of the work (the scores on the summaries) turned out to be the best recorded that year for any senior English assignment. Furthermore, the skills the students were engaged in—listening, note taking, and writing—were directly tied to the goals of the senior English class.

The best aspect of interviews and surveys is that they provide you, as a teacher researcher, with the actual voices and the precise words of your respondents. Later, when reporting on your data, this type of information will add credibility to your findings and vitality to your reports.

Note: Occasionally action researchers have found themselves in trouble because they didn't explain precisely how the data would be used before soliciting respondents' cooperation. For this reason, you should always tell your respondents how you plan to use the information they provide and whether, or when, you plan to make a summary of your data available.

Chapters 7 and 8 have presented information on many helpful forms of data collection for action research. Each of these techniques is powerful enough to provide you with helpful insights into the dynamics of teaching and learning in your school or classroom. However, most teacher researchers want more than helpful insights from all their efforts; they want findings that will inspire confidence. The next chapter looks at how you can develop a comprehensive and cohesive plan for data collection. You will learn how triangulation and the strategies described earlier can surface valid and reliable answers to the questions that triggered your research in the first place.

9 Data Collection: Building a Valid and Reliable Data Collection Plan

Chapters 7 and 8 introduced a variety of viable data collection techniques. However, employing proven techniques doesn't guarantee the quality of the findings that emerge. The reality is, action research simply isn't worth doing unless it is done well. Although that may sound like just an old refrain, it is far more. The imperative for maintaining high standards of quality is a truth learned and sometimes painfully relearned by teacher researchers. There are three fundamental reasons why you as a teacher researcher should hold yourself to the highest quality standards possible:

1. Your obligation to students
2. The need for personal and collective efficacy
3. The need to add to the professional knowledge base

The first reason, your obligation to students, rests on the premise that the education of the community's young is a sacred trust placed upon you as a educator. Therefore, the decisions you make on behalf of students are actions of no small consequence. No one, least of all teachers, would wish to see students victimized by malpractice. When you make teaching decisions on the basis of sloppy research, you place your students at risk.

A second reason to hold your action research to the highest standards of quality is that understanding your influence on educational outcomes can significantly enhance your personal and collective feelings of efficacy. However, before you can take credit for the success reflected in your data, the quality of that data must withstand the scrutiny of the world's most critical jury—your own skeptical mind. Ultimately, if you doubt your own conclusions regarding the contribution you have made to your students, those findings won't have much impact on your feelings of self-worth.

The third factor, adding to the knowledge base, may not seem important if you are a teacher researcher practicing in a one-room school or you find yourself in a school culture that emphasizes individualism. However, it should be extremely relevant to the vast majority of teachers—those of you who tend to share what you've learned with your colleagues. Not infrequently, one of the unspoken reasons for conducting action research is to persuade or entice your skeptical colleagues to consider "your" perspective on an issue. When you present your research to peers who are skeptical about the theory you are following, you should expect a similar skepticism about the research findings you produce concerning those theories. If your pedagogical opponents can find fatal flaws in your action research data, all future efforts at persuasion become that much more difficult.

Quality Criteria

The criteria used to establish the quality of action research should be no different from those used with other forms of research. Topping any researcher's list of quality criteria are the twin pillars of science: *validity* and *reliability*, first introduced in Chapter 1. These concepts are so critical to the quality of action research that it is worth taking some time to discuss and explore each of them.

Validity

As you no doubt recall from Education Psychology 101, *validity* refers to the essential truthfulness of a piece of data. By asserting validity, the researcher is asserting that the data actually measure or reflect the specific phenomenon claimed. Scientific history is full of examples of research findings that were discredited because they were shown to lack validity.

A mercury thermometer is an example of a valid instrument yielding valid data. The height reached by the fluid in an accurate thermometer is a valid and appropriate measurement of air temperature. Similarly, the movement of a membrane in a barometer is an appropriate and valid way to determine barometric pressure. A ruler can be a valid way to measure length, and unfortunately (for those of us who are weight conscious) a bathroom scale can be a valid measure of weight.

Nothing has helped me understand the importance of attending to validity as much as my experience with performance assessment. One of the great accomplishments of the modern assessment movement has been drawing teacher attention to the value of *authentic work* products. Although bubble-sheet tests can, in many cases, produce valid data, teachers' preference for authentic work products is understandable. It is analogous to historians' preference for "primary source material" over "secondary source material." Intuitively, we all know that words from the horse's mouth are more believable than words related by the horse's trainer. Similarly, a piece of actual student writing has more validity than a score obtained on the language section of a standardized multiple-choice exam. A performance by the school band is a better indicator of students' ability to execute a musical piece than are the students' grades in band.

However, even given the deserved popularity of performance and portfolio assessments, these types of data are not exempt from concerns regarding validity. For example, how should we react to the use of a written lab report as a means to assess student understanding of the scientific method? Should a lab report written in standard English be accepted as a valid indicator of a student's understanding of science?

Suppose you answered yes. Would you still accept that lab report as a valid indicator if you learned that the student lacked fluency in English? Probably not. This is because the English-language proficiency needed to complete the report introduced what scientists call an *intervening and confounding variable*. In the case of assessing the proficiency in science of a student with limited English proficiency, the written aspect of the report intervenes and thereby confounds the accuracy of the assessment. Intervening and confounding variables are factors that get in the way of valid assessment. This is why when conducting assessments on student learning and collecting data for action research, it is important to ask:

> *Are there any factors or intervening variables that should cause me to distrust these data?*

Reliability

Reliability is a different but no less important concept. Reliability relates to researchers' claims regarding the accuracy of their data. A few years ago, when a police officer issued me a ticket for speeding, I didn't question the validity of his using an expensive, city-issued speedometer. I was willing to concede to the officer the validity of measuring vehicular speed with a speedometer. However, I urged him to consider my thesis regarding the reliability of his speedometer. I respectfully suggested that although I knew he sincerely believed that his speedometer was accurate, he ought to consider the possibility that it could be damaged. I argued that if it were broken it wouldn't produce an accurate, credible, and reliable measure of my speed. What I was suggesting was that although speedometers are valid measures of speed, they aren't always reliable.

Unfortunately, I lost that argument. I fared no better when I presented the same "reasonable doubt" plea to the judge. Unbeknownst to me, the state police regularly establish the reliability (accuracy) of their speedometers by testing the speedometer on each patrol car every morning. In the end, I had to pay the fine. But in return I learned a memorable lesson on the value of establishing reliability.

Reliability problems in education often arise when researchers overstate the importance of data drawn from too small or too restricted a sample. For example, imagine if when I was a high school principal I claimed to the school board that I had evidence that the parents love our school's programs. When the board chair asked me how I could make such a claim, I responded by defensively asserting it was a conclusion based on "hard data"—specifically, a survey taken at the last winter band banquet. The board chair might respond that because that event was attended by only 5 percent of the school's parents and all the parents who attended had one thing in common—they had children in band—my conclusions were "unreliable." He would be right. Claiming that such a small and select sample accurately represented the views of a total population (all the school's parents) stretches the credibility of my assertion well beyond reasonableness.

To enhance the reliability of your action research data, you need to continually ask yourself these questions when planning data collection:

- *Is this information an accurate representation of reality?*
- *Can I think of any reasons to be suspicious of its accuracy?*

Establishing Validity and Reliability

To appreciate the concepts of validity and reliability and how you might establish them, consider how you would behave as a juror deliberating in a criminal trial. Lawyers for both sides would argue their cases as persuasively as possible. Your task as a juror is to determine which of the arguments to believe. In deciding if a lawyer had "proved the case," you would probably ask these questions regarding validity: Are these claims credible? Can I truly believe that this evidence means what these witnesses and lawyers say it does? To determine the reliability of the evidence, you would ask questions such as these about the accuracy of the witnesses' recollections and testimony: Can I trust the accuracy of their eyes and ears? Could time or emotions have played a trick on their memories?

So how do legal "researchers"—defense lawyers and prosecutors—convince a jury of the essential truth and accuracy (validity and reliability) of their cases? They do it through the twin processes of *corroboration* and *impeachment*. When they want the jury to believe what one of their witnesses said, they bring in other independent witnesses. If an additional witness *corroborates* everything the first witness said, it increases the confidence a juror will have in the initial testimony. The more independent pieces of evidence a lawyer can place before a jury, the more the jurors will trust the truthfulness and accuracy of the claims. Conversely, if lawyers want the jury to doubt the truth and accuracy (validity and reliability) of the other side, they try to *impeach* (challenge the credibility of) the testimony of the other side, by, for example, entering into evidence alternative or irreconcilable reports on the same phenomenon from several independent sources.

Triangulation

Action researchers use a similar process to that used by lawyers. It is called *triangulation*, and, as was discussed in Chapters 1 and 2, it involves the use of multiple independent sources of data to establish the truth and accuracy of a claim.

There are ways to develop valid and reliable instruments without triangulation, but these methods are often problematic. First, they are time-consuming and frequently prohibitive in terms of cost. This is because significant field-testing is required to establish the validity and reliability of a measuring instrument. Just consider the many millions of dollars invested by publishers to support the validity and reliability of their standardized tests. But even if teachers were willing to invest the time, money, and energy required to establish technical validity (construct and content) for their home-grown instruments, they probably wouldn't be happy with what they produced.

For good reason, educators are intuitively unimpressed with "single instrument measures." They tend to question whether any single tool could ever capture the full reality of any meaningful educational outcome. Occasionally I will meet a layperson who believes that SAT scores alone (or another piece of seemingly compelling data, such as college admissions data or discipline referrals) provide an accurate picture of a school's quality. But I have never met a knowledgeable educator who is willing to make a judgment based upon any of those same valid and reliable instruments. This is because educators know that what these "valid and reliable" instruments reveal is simply too narrow to justify conclusions regarding educational quality.

This is not to say that these instruments (SAT scores, college admissions, discipline referrals, and so forth) aren't valuable windows into the larger phenomenon (the quality of a school), but before conclusions can be drawn about the big picture, those findings need to be corroborated by looking at the phenomenon through a variety of other windows.

Figure 9.1 illustrates what a plan for triangulated data collection might look like to answer a question on the quality of a high school.

Although we might be skeptical about drawing conclusions regarding a school's quality from any one of the success indicators in Figure 9.1, if all of these instruments painted a similar picture, we would, no doubt, feel confident in declaring the school "good."

FIGURE 9.1

A Plan for Triangulated Data Collection

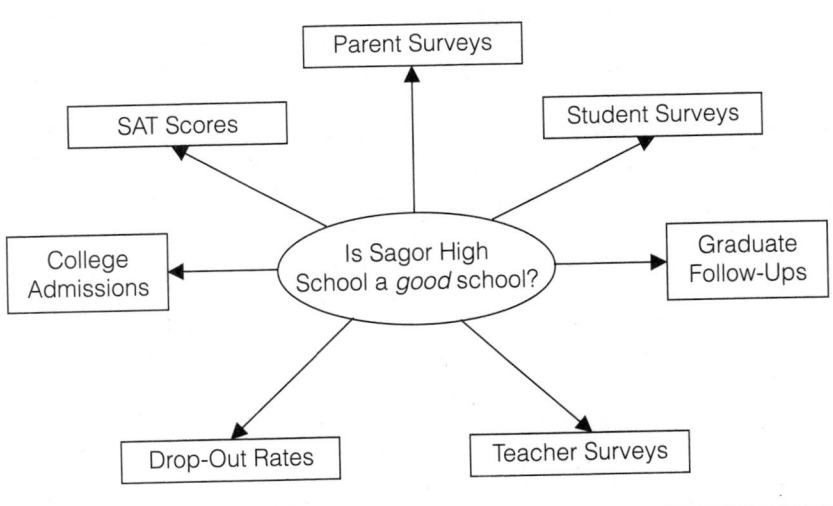

Finishing the Research Proposal

Chapter 6 presented guidelines for producing a written problem statement/research proposal (Implementation Strategy #6). The sample proposal written by Richard and Georgia, although short, contained all the items expected from a formal research proposal except the data collection plan. Chapter 2 described the triangulation matrix as a helpful planning tool (Figure 2.3, p. 21). Figure 9.2 shows the triangulated data collection plan, in the form of a matrix, that Richard and Georgia used to answer their research questions. Implementation Strategy #10 can help you complete a triangulation matrix.

FIGURE 9.2

Triangulation Matrix for Real World Advocacy Project Research Questions

Research Question	Data Source #1	Data Source #2	Data Source #3
1. Could we motivate our 8th graders to conduct and complete Real World Advocacy Projects?	Teacher journals	Student surveys	Grade book records
2. What would be the quality of the projects produced by our students?	Teacher assessments using a project rubric	Student self-assessments using the same rubric	Assessment by community members using the rubric
3. Would the completion of Real World Advocacy Projects result in enhanced feelings of social efficacy for our students?	Surveys of students' other teachers	Interviews with random sample of students	Interviews with random sample of parents

Implementation Strategy #10—
Building a Triangulated Data Collection Plan

WHAT:
Constructing a data collection plan with high probability of producing valid and reliable answers to your research questions

HOW:
1. Prepare a four-column data collection matrix with separate rows for each research question (see Figure 9.2).

2. Write your research questions in column 1 of your matrix.

3. For each research question, ask yourself the following: What is one source of data that could help answer this question? Write your answer in column 2 next to the research question.

4. Ask the question two more times to determine a second and third source of data, and write your answers in columns 3 and 4, respectively.*

5. Repeat this process for each research question.

6. Review the completed matrix and ask yourself the following question: Are these the best sources of data I/we could collect in answer to each of these questions? When you are satisfied with your answer to this question, you have a completed data collection plan.

*Although this strategy suggests collecting three types of data to answer a research question, it is perfectly permissible to collect more than three types.

A Last Important Step

Once you have developed a triangulated data collection plan, you have accomplished much of the hard work of action research. Most doctoral students report that the hardest aspect of completing a doctorate is getting a comprehensive research proposal through their dissertation committee. Once the rationale for their research has been established and a methodology (the data collection plan) for answering their research questions has been put in place, all that is left is to carry out the proposal.

If you, alone or with colleagues, have followed the steps outlined in this book thus far, you are ready to proceed. Now all you have to do is carry out your plan.

Unfortunately, many beginning action researchers stall at this point, usually because completing the next stage, data collection, requires budgeting time from an already packed schedule. To get over this hurdle, it is helpful to commit to a time line and a process for completing the work of data collection. The rationale for formalizing this commitment is to keep the demands of a hectic work life from getting in the way of completing what should prove to be a most satisfying piece of work. Implementation Strategy #11 takes only a few minutes to complete, but doing so will help ensure that you get over the time hurdle and maintain your momentum for completing your research.

Implementation Strategy #11— Data Collection Time Line/To-Do List

WHAT:
Making a commitment to a plan for completing the data collection portion of your action research

HOW:
1. Make a four-column list on a sheet of chart paper.

2. Brainstorm (either individually or, if your research is a team effort, with your colleagues) a list of each thing that needs to be accomplished in order to complete your triangulated data collection plan. List these items (roughly in chronological order) in the left-hand column on the chart paper.

3. In the second column, write the date that each should be accomplished. Then ask yourself if it is realistic to complete this item by that date. If the answer is yes, go to the next item. If the answer is no, determine the earliest "realistic" date.

4. If working individually, go on to the next step. If working as a team, go through each item on the list and determine who is willing to be responsible to see that this item is accomplished by the agreed upon date. Write that person's name in column 3.

5. Ask yourself (or ask the team) the following question: What types of support or help might I/we need to complete each of these items? Perhaps you will need some support from your principal or some help from a professor at a local university. Write the name of the person or organization whose help you anticipate needing in the last column and commit to a time for making contact with these "critical friends."

6. One last time, ask yourself or your team if this plan is realistic. If you answer yes, you are ready to proceed. If you answer no, repeat this strategy.

. . . .

Chapters 10 and 11 explore the three remaining steps in the action research process: data analysis, reporting, and action planning. Chapter 12 discusses a number of important ethical and methodological issues that will be particularly helpful for beginning researchers. If you intend to conduct your data collection before reading the rest of this book, I strongly recommend that you read Chapter 12 first.

10 Making Sense of the Data

Once you have carried out a triangulated data collection plan and have all the data you had hoped for, it is time to start making meaning out of it all. It is likely that some of your data are quantitative (test scores, attendance data, and so on) and some are qualitative (journals, interview transcripts, student portfolios, and so on). On the surface it may look like quite a hodgepodge. In this chapter you will learn how to apply a generic process for making sense of this disparate data.

The What and Why of Data Analysis

Some may argue that in order to truly understand a phenomenon, there is no acceptable substitute for personally reviewing all the relevant data. This assertion holds more than a little truth. Returning to the jury analogy from the previous example, if we were to arrive at a verdict in a criminal trial, the parties to the dispute would expect us to consider every available piece of evidence when we deliberated on the guilt or innocence of the defendant. However, in the business of real life, few of us have the time to review every piece of pertinent material related to the myriad tasks before us. This usually isn't a problem, because most of us have consciously or subconsciously developed a reliance on dependable sources to synthesize this information for us. To illustrate this point, let's consider two synthesizers many of us rely on—the news reporter and the history teacher.

The News Reporter

If we, as citizens, wanted to fully understand what is happening with a piece of legislation before Congress, we would need to review each of the statements, predilections, and biases of the 535 senators and representatives. Furthermore, we would find it helpful to review the history of similar pieces of legislation faced by this and past Congresses. And finally, because legislating is an ever-evolving process, it would be important to examine these data over time to provide more than a one-day snapshot of congressional attitudes and posturing. It's likely that very few of us are ready, willing, and able to make such a commitment in order to meet our responsibilities as citizens. Instead, most of us rely on the reporters and pundits whom we trust to provide us with an accurate picture of what is transpiring miles away from our busy lives.

Before looking at how reporters carry out their duties, it's helpful to review the two primary questions that should guide researchers when conducting data analysis:

- What is the story embedded in my data?
- What factors significantly influenced this story?

As discussed in earlier, credible (i.e., valid and reliable) answers to those two questions are unlikely to be found in the words of any single respondent and probably won't be captured by any single instrument. Returning to the example of congressional action, we are well aware of the risks involved when we rely solely on the public statements of our legislators. For various reasons, both positive and negative, we need to take the public pronouncements of politicians, uncorroborated by other evidence, with more than a grain of salt. This is why in politics, as well as in action research, triangulation becomes so important. It is not enough to know what politicians are saying; we also need to know about their past behavior in similar situations and the pressures they are likely to encounter in the future. Only when we consider all of these factors can we confidently predict what will likely transpire next. This brings us to the essential role of the Capitol Hill correspondent.

Unlike most citizens, these correspondents work and live in the Washington, D.C., area. They have personal experience with and access to reliable data on the history of each individual legislator and the Congress as a whole. They are privy to many public and private discussions held by policymakers on each pending piece of legislation. If they do their job correctly, they use this mountain of data to provide us with valuable insights into the forces that will affect, in the near and long term, those making the decisions. The reporter's job is to put this triangulated data together, analyze it, and then share the results with us. By doing so, they fulfill both functions of analysis: they provide us with their understanding of the story as well as their insights into the phenomena behind the story. We can then sit back at home and hear their analysis as summarized on the evening news. For example, we might turn on the news and hear something like this:

> No one in Congress seems willing to talk on the record about the impending insolvency of the Social Security and Medicare trust funds. The majority party appears to be unwilling to make any sincere efforts to bring this legislation to the floor for a vote. Meanwhile, the minority party isn't applying any pressure to force the issue. It seems as if this Congress would rather pretend that this hot issue doesn't exist, at least until after election day.

That 20-second statement accomplishes the first (and perhaps easiest) aspect of data analysis: describing the story. It tells us what is going on and it does so succinctly. Why is it credible? For one thing, the researcher/reporter shares with us the data that led to their conclusion. That 20-second segment tells us that data from the following sources informed the reporter's story:

• The public behavior of the majority leadership (not talking on the record)

• The public behavior of the minority leadership (silent on the issue)

• The private behavior of the majority leadership (not scheduling a vote)

• The private behavior of the minority leadership (not applying pressure for a vote)

The second reason this story seems credible is that we believe that this reporter is in a good "position" to know the facts. She gained our confidence because of her location, her ability to engage in daily off-the-record discussions with key policymakers, as well as her opportunity to observe legislative action firsthand.

At this point the reporter might move on to address the second role of analysis: to help illuminate the phenomena that influenced the story:

> Chances for passage of significant Social Security reform legislation is unlikely this session primarily because, even if it is good policy, it is bad politics. With both parties looking ahead to the upcoming presidential election, neither side wishes to alienate the ever-increasing segment of the electorate that is elderly or retired. Observing the behavior of the ranking members of the House and Senate at hearings this week, it seemed apparent that with the predicted high turnout (over 75 percent of eligible senior citizens are projected to vote) and the depth of the anxiety of

people living on fixed incomes (as reported last night by the recent XYZ News poll) regarding the spiraling costs of health care and housing, passage of meaningful reform is perceived as equivalent to political suicide, especially for the 435 Representatives and 33 Senators facing election.

Why should we choose to trust this reporter's explanation (analysis)? There might be several reasons. First, as mentioned earlier, we are probably impressed by the fact that she based her conclusions on a variety of data sources (triangulation) and alluded to those sources in her report. Specifically, her conclusions were influenced by

- Personal observations
- Voting patterns (particularly of the elderly and those with fixed incomes)
- Past congressional behavior
- Recent public opinion polls

The second reason relates to our experience. We are likely to trust her judgment this time provided her past analyses have been accurate. Finally, and perhaps most important, we invest confidence in her report because each piece of data that she cited in support of her conclusions is a piece of data that we could, if we so desired, verify independently and subject to our own analysis.

Historians

We often hear folks say, "I wonder what history will say about this?" or "History tells us . . ." Why are we willing to trust in the reports of people (historians, in particular) who may not have been alive during the episodes they are writing about? Why do we look at history as containing reasonable approximations of truth, rather than seeing it as simply the fictitious ramblings of eloquent writers?

The answer may lie in our intuitive understanding of the processes used by honest historians as they do their work. They examine primary sources (when available), they review the work (data) of other historians, and they report in detail on the pieces of the jigsaw puzzle that they see coming together to tell a compelling story. Furthermore, as with the news reporter, the historical record (the raw data) they used to inform their judgments is available in the archives to anyone who is willing to spend the time to draw their own conclusions.

Applying These Lessons to the Analysis of Action Research

The same principles used by fair-minded historians and ethical journalists apply to action researchers. As action researchers, we should

- Review the relevant research literature.
- Report accurate and adequate descriptive accounts about the context we are reporting on.
- Share or make all the raw data available for analysis by others, if and when desired.

Ultimately (unless we teach in an isolated one-room schoolhouse), we will share our research, formally or informally, with our colleagues. For this reason you should view yourself (when in your researcher role) as a "service provider" for your teaching colleagues. Just as historians and reporters provide us, the consumers of their analyses, with a service, so do action researchers. As a school-based action researcher, I suggest that you consider yourself as the "executive secretary" for a busy network of practitioners.

For a variety of reasons, your colleagues aren't likely willing to spend a lot of time looking at and reviewing all of the raw data. They probably would prefer to have someone else analyze the data and then share their review of the findings and conclusions.

Students of school administration will appreciate the importance of the executive secretary role, which is the role played by a school district superintendent. The superintendent's job is to serve as the executive secretary for a part-time, elected board of education. Board members have neither the time, the expertise, nor the interest to work full time on the myriad daily details that confront the school district. That is why they hire a superintendent. They want the superintendent to be intimately aware of everything going on; they then expect the superintendent to provide them with a concise summary of the important data and to be prepared to explain its relevance so that they, the board members, are able to do their job—setting district policy.

The history of the superintendency illustrates why analysis is such a high-stakes business. If and when a board of education has reason to doubt the credibility of the analysis they are getting from their executive secretary (the superintendent), they will send that superintendent packing. For action researchers, historians, reporters, executive secretaries, and school superintendents, the confidence and credibility that our "customers" invest in our research summaries is everything!

Deciding What to Include

Raw data can be enormous in scope. Report cards, portfolios, teacher grade books, classroom behavior, standardized test results, for example—when these are all multiplied by, for example, 500 students, the sheer scope of the data we've collected can be overwhelming!

In many ways the task for the busy action researcher appears no more (or less) complex than the problem that a disorganized worker like me faces on a regular basis when trying to make sense of a messy and cluttered desk. As it turns out, the process of making meaning out of what appears to be chaos has become remarkably simple for me. My system of office organization is "piles." When my office becomes cluttered to the point that I can hardly get through the door, I realize that clearing up this mess is prerequisite for getting organized. I begin the organizing task by sifting through every piece of paper and putting it into categories that later become piles. For example, one pile may relate to the classes I'm currently teaching; another pile may contain stuff requiring immediate attention; another might contain material I want to share with others; and one may consist of student papers needing to be corrected.

After several hours of sifting, sorting, and piling, some things begin to become apparent (much as research findings begin to surface). For example, I might find that

- I am way behind in grading and returning papers.
- It is no wonder that my creditors keep calling me, as I am also far behind in paying my bills, filing my travel reimbursements, and taking care of other onerous paperwork.
- If my friends are ever going to appreciate my saving stuff to share with them, perhaps I should send this material in a more timely manner.

I could blissfully ignore those findings as long as they stayed lost in the mass (or should I say mess?) of raw data on my desk. However, once these data were categorized and sorted into piles, I could no longer ignore those conclusions.

Coding and Characterizing Action Research Data

Sorting into categories is the first and most important step in the data analysis process. This part of the process is called *coding*. Codes are numbers, symbols, or letters corresponding to the categories (piles) into which the data will be sorted. The specific sequence of the process follows. Implementation Strategy #12 (pp. 127–128) will succinctly guide you through these steps.

1. Assemble all the data that you think might illuminate the issue or question you are researching. (These are the data collected in accordance with your data collection matrix).

2. Skim the data with pen and notepad in hand, being sure that you are in a relaxed and open frame of mind. If you are distracted by other concerns, leave this step to another time. Your job is to consider any and all possible categories for sorting.

3. Create your categories. Whenever you see repetition or a pattern seems to be emerging, jot a name for that category or pattern on a notepad.

4. When you've finished skimming the data and believe you have a fairly complete list of categories into which your data might be sorted, you are ready to do your coding/sorting.

5. Create "bins" for your data. Matt Miles and Michael Huberman (1994) coined the term bins to refer to the piles into which data could be placed. The term brings to mind an image of what I do every evening with the recyclables in our house. I remove from the corner of our kitchen table the undifferentiated data on the Sagor family's consumption habits (a mass of paper, metal, glass, and plastic) and take it to the garage, where I sort it into six color-coded bins provided by the recycling company: one each for plastic, newsprint, other paper/cardboard, colored glass, clear glass, and metal.

6. Once you have identified your bins, reread the data attaching a code (corresponding to the appropriate bin) on every pertinent item. This can be done in a variety of ways. You could

- Put a number or letter code in a margin next to the item.
- Highlight all similar items with the same color highlighter.
- Rewrite the item (or a brief identifying description of the item) on an index card and place it into a physical bin, or pile.
- Create a computerized list of the items, inserting a code number or letter before each item.

7. Now it's time to place all similarly coded data in a single location. This generally means retyping the data or using a word processor to re-sort the data by assigned code. (Most word processors are programmed to do this task automatically.)

8. Look for significant trends. In the recycling example, when my raw data were sitting on the kitchen counter, all that I could conclude was that we consumed lots of stuff. But after sorting it into the bins, I realized that the bin for colored glass was overflowing with empty beverage

bottles and that the newsprint bin was piled high with unopened newspapers.

9. Prepare a list of tentative findings from the trends you observed. After sorting several days' worth of family recyclables I can state with authority that we consume an enormous amount of beverages and that although we can say quite accurately that we subscribe to many newspapers, it also appears that we fail to read most of them. I might summarize my insights from the data on my family's recyclables in this way:

a. My expanding waistline, which I had blamed on a lack of exercise, might instead be attributable to my soft drink consumption.

b. Our family should budget more time for reading our daily newspapers or cancel some subscriptions.

Let's leave the recycling example behind and return to Georgia and Richard's study of the Real World Advocacy Project (RWAP). How did the coding process work for them? As you may recall, they had three research questions and used three independent sources of data to answer each question.

Research Question #1: Could we motivate our 8th graders to conduct and complete Real World Advocacy Projects? As Georgia and Richard skimmed the data they had collected in response to this question, they decided to create two bins for their data: one for low student motivation and one that reflected high levels of motivation. Then they put their data on index cards. The data they were sorting were of three types: statistical data (for example, percentage of assignments completed on time before the RWAP project, as well as percentage completed during the RWAP project); verbatim data (quotes drawn from student surveys, from teacher journals, parent interviews, and so forth); and "factoids," statements of fact drawn from trends observed in teacher grade books and from school records (for example, 100 percent of the students completed their RWAP on time, 40 percent of the students received a D in social studies the year before).

Research Question #2: What would be the quality of the projects produced by our students? The data to answer this question came from a statistical analysis of the data on the quality of the RWAP projects. These data had been gathered using the rubric/scoring guide developed for that purpose (Figure 7.6). Georgia and Richard decided to sort these data by source: one bin for teacher assessments, a second bin for student assessments, and a third bin for assessments from the external assessors. They then decided to rank the projects based on scores awarded. Figure 10.1 (p. 129) shows this rank ordering. Displaying the data this way serves another valuable purpose. It enabled Georgia and Richard to determine whether their data fulfilled the goal of inter-rater reliability.

    Research Question #3: *Would the completion of Real World Advocacy Projects result in enhanced feelings of social efficacy for our students?* To determine the bins necessary for analyzing these data, the researchers not only skimmed surveys, journals, and interview transcripts, but they went back to their original problem statement and theory (graphic reconstruction) to see if the theories they developed during the problem-formulation phase turned out to be supportable by these data. The bins they decided to use were

- Reactions of decision makers
- Reactions of parents
- Reactions of other teachers
- Future plans
- Power (efficacy) statements
- Powerless (low efficacy) statements

    Regardless of the focus of the inquiry, sorting one's data into bins is a helpful first step for data analysis. The steps outlined in Implementation Strategy 12 should help you code the data collected for each research question.

Implementation Strategy #12—Coding Data for Analysis

WHAT:
A means to sort, organize, and characterize accumulated data

WHEN:
After completion of the data collection process

HOW:
1. Assemble all the data that you or your group collected.

2. Individually skim the data looking for possible categories for sorting.

3. Create categories; if and when a pattern emerges, write a name for that pattern on a notepad.

4. Complete your list of categories. When everyone has completed skimming the data, discuss the categories on your lists and agree to a set of categories for sorting the data.

5. Reread the data, placing a code (corresponding to the appropriate category) on each pertinent item. This can be done in any of the following ways:

- Put a number or letter code in a margin.
- Highlight all similar items with the same color highlighter.
- Rewrite the item on an index card and place it into a physical bin.
- Create a computerized list of the items, inserting a code number or letter before each item.

6. Put all similarly coded data in a single location. This generally means retyping or using your computer to re-sort all the data by code.

7. Summarize trends and insights. Review the data in each category and generate a list of tentative factual assertions that are supported by the data in that category. Note: These tentative assertions may be quantitative (for example, "80 percent of the journals examined contained positive comments about the teacher") or qualitative (for example, "It appeared that for the first time these students understood the political process").

Using an Analysis Matrix to Sift Through Bins

Occasionally the first cut at sorting data produces satisfactory results, but often it does not. It is important to keep in mind that the first purpose of analysis is to uncover the story buried in the data. Sometimes the story is quite elusive, and you need to sort and re-sort and ultimately come up with new bins or categories to determine what is actually going on. Of course, sometimes the real story is that "nothing was going on." Don't be disappointed if that happens. You can learn as much by discovering which of your theories didn't work as by discovering which theories did.

Occasionally you will find that your bins or categories were too broad and need to be subdivided. Sometimes you realize that your bins or categories were too narrow and could be combined to show a clearer picture of reality. As a researcher you need to keep playing with the data: re-sorting, reconfiguring, and rearranging until you are sure that you have given "the story" every possible chance to emerge.

Figure 10.1

Rankings of Real World Advocacy Projects and Determination of Inter-Rater Reliability

Project	Teacher Rating	Community Member Rating	Student Self-Assessment
Park Development	20	20	20
Athletic Policies	20	19	18
Animal Cruelty	15	20	14
Skateboard Regulation	18	18	16
Discipline Appeals	17	18	15
Bike Lanes	17	18	15
Homework Fairness	17	17	15
Playground Equipment	16	16	14
Community Center	16	16	14
Field Trips	16	15	13
Leash Laws	16	15	13
Activity Buses	16	15	13
Girls' Sports	16	15	12
School Lunches	16	14	11
Locker Assignments	15	14	11
Reform Teacher Advisory Program	12	13	10

In many cases the coding and sorting of data is helpful, but it's not enough to "free the story." At this point, a two-dimensional analysis matrix can help you further subdivide and analyze the data. All that's required is a large sheet of poster paper and a pad of Post-it notes. Across the top of paper, write the names of each of the bins into which you have already sorted your data. Next, you need to decide on the best way to subdivide the data. These will become the rows along the side of the matrix. There are many alternatives, depending on the focus of your study. Among the possibilities are

- Types of data (surveys, interviews, test scores)
- Sources of data (students, parents, teachers)
- Individual subjects or cases (particular students or groups of students)
- Categories of subjects (gender, ethnicity, disabilities, etc.)
- Time frames (fall, winter, spring)

Then take each piece of data from the bins, rewrite it on a Post-it note, and place the note in the appropriate cell on the matrix.

The final step in the process is to look carefully at your data analysis matrix and ask yourself (and your partners, if you are part of a team), "Are there relevant facts that we know emerged from our data that haven't shown up in any of the cells?" I call these types of facts "factoids." Write all relevant factoids on Post-it notes and place them in the appropriate cells of the analysis matrix. After adding the factoids, your analysis matrix is complete.

Here's how Richard and Georgia developed their analysis matrix. At the top of their sheet of paper they wrote these labels:

- Evidence of motivation
- Evidence of detachment
- Evidence of enjoyment
- Evidence of empowerment
- Evidence of behavior change
- Contrast with previous work

After considering a number of possibilities, Richard and Georgia elected to sort their data by project. The listing of the 16 projects later became the rows for the matrix. Figure 10.2 illustrates the finished structure of the matrix that Richard and Georgia used for their analysis.

As they began re-sorting the data in the motivation bin, Georgia and Richard found this comment from Jorge's mother: "If he applied himself to all his schoolwork like he has to this assignment, he would be

FIGURE 10.2

An Analysis Matrix—Developing Social Efficacy

Project	Evidence of Motivation	Evidence of Detachment	Evidence of Enjoyment	Evidence of Empowerment	Evidence of Behavior Change	Contrast with Previous Work
Park Development						
Athletic Policies						
Animal Cruelty						
Skateboard Regulation						
Discipline Appeals						
Bike Lanes						
Homework Fairness						
Playground Equipment						
Community Center						

FIGURE 10.2—*continued*

An Analysis Matrix—Developing Social Efficacy

Project	Evidence of Motivation	Evidence of Detachment	Evidence of Enjoyment	Evidence of Empowerment	Evidence of Behavior Change	Contrast with Previous Work
Field Trips						
Leash Laws						
Activity Buses						
Girls' Sports						
School Lunches						
Locker Assignments						
Teacher Advisory						

an *A* student." They wrote the comment on a Post-it note and affixed it to the matrix in the cell labeled "motivation" (at the top) and Skateboard Regulation (Jorge's project) on the side.

Among the factoids that Richard and Georgia put on the RWAP data analysis matrix were these:

• The park development project received perfect scores from all assessors.

• The teacher advisory project had to be rewritten twice to achieve a satisfactory grade.

List of Findings

At this point it is a good idea to create a list, in no particular order, of the findings that emerged from the matrix. These findings are narrative, factual statements that popped out while you were sorting the data. Here are the list of findings (organized by research questions) from Richard and Georgia's study:

Question #1: Could we motivate our 8th graders to conduct and complete Real World Advocacy Projects?

• 112 (78 percent) of teacher journal entries reflected at least one positive comment regarding student motivation.

• 46 (32 percent) of teacher journal entries made reference to a concern about student commitment.

• 85 percent of the references reflected "motivation."

• 19 percent of the references reflected "detachment."

• All negative teacher comments were focused on 7 out of the 120 students.

• Most of those negative observations were recorded during the first six weeks of the term.

• During the last six weeks, only five negative observations were reported by the two teachers.

• 118 of the 120 students (98 percent) rated their enjoyment of the project with a score of 8 or higher.

• Two students rated the RWAP assignment as a 5 (average) on the 10-point enjoyment scale.

• 115 of the 120 students (96 percent) rated their personal effort as 8 or above.

• One student reported his effort as less than 5.

• 100 percent of the students reported interest in doing this again.

- All 120 students completed their RWAP project.
- On the six previous assignments, the completion rate was 72 percent.
- All 17 projects met or exceeded the 12-point minimum score established for credit.
- One project had to be revised in order to obtain the minimum score of 12.

Question #2: What would be the quality of the projects produced by our students?

- A significant degree of "inter-rater reliability" was obtained with the scoring guides.
- The "absolute" standards applied by the three sets of evaluators were different.
- The teachers tended to award higher scores for most projects than did students or outsiders.
- For 16 of the 17 projects, the "relative rankings" of the three groups of evaluators were consistent.
- In most cases the students tended to be tougher on themselves than either their teachers or the community assessors.

Question #3: Would the completion of Real World Advocacy Projects result in enhanced feelings of social efficacy for our students?

- In over one-third of the teacher interviews, the respondents were unable to recall any conversations or behavior changes attributable to the RWAP assignment.
- When teachers did recall hearing something about the RWAP project (62 percent), the things shared were positive.
- 95 percent of the 475 coded interview comments indicated a positive statement or behavior regarding the Real World Advocacy Project.
- 45 of the 50 parents interviewed (90 percent) were able to cite specific statements regarding the project made at home by their students.
- Four parents reported negative comments.
- All but one of the students interviewed said the project contributed to seeing how they can make a difference. The one student who disagreed could have been scored either way.

Draft Summary Assertions

Your list of narrative statements of findings should be nonevaluative and nonjudgmental. Now it is time to move into your executive secretary role and summarize what you believe you have learned from your findings in response to each of your research questions. These understandings are called "summary assertions." These are the assertions Georgia and Richard came up with:

• **Summary Assertion (Question #1):** Based upon our data, we feel comfortable in asserting that our 8th grade civics students demonstrated the requisite motivation to conduct, complete, and produce quality products through the RWAP.

• **Summary Assertion (Question #2):** It is important to note that although the RWAP projects had a significant range in quality (mean scores of 12.2–20.0), no projects were scored as falling below the satisfactory level (12.0). Therefore, we conclude that our students had, in fact, succeeded at the goal of producing quality projects.

• **Summary Assertion (Question #3):** Our analysis of the interviews led us to believe the Real World Advocacy Project had an impact on students' feelings of social efficacy. We are, however, concerned that the wording of the interview questions might have suggested to the students what answers we were looking for.

Implementation Strategy #13: Using a Matrix for Data Analysis

WHAT:
A tool for surfacing the story or stories that may be buried in the data

HOW:
1. Across the top of a long sheet of paper, write column headings corresponding to the title of each data collection "bin."

2. As a group, discuss the possible ways that the data in the bins could be categorized: subjects, dates, types of data, and so on.

3. When you agree on a way to subdivide the data, write the appropriate row labels on the vertical axis of the matrix.

4. Reread the data in each bin, rewrite each piece of data on a Post-it note, and place it in the appropriate cell of the matrix.

5. Write summary findings (supportable by these and other data), also called "factoids," on the appropriate place on the matrix, noting the source of the factoid.

6. Summarize the story or stories revealed by your matrix with a list of findings and tentative assertions.

Member Checking

Often at this point, when data analysis is nearly complete, action researchers want to provide additional validity to their findings. One fast and efficient way to accomplish this is through a simple process that qualitative researchers call "member checking." Member checking can add real power to research findings. In short, member checking is asking the members of the population being studied for their reaction to the findings. In her book *The Good High School* (1983), Sara Lawrence Lightfoot uses an artistic metaphor to describe this process. She likens her findings (chapter-length written descriptions of her visits to schools) to portraits. Like an artist who has finished a family portrait, she hands her piece of work over to her model and asks for a reaction. If a family (school community) who had their picture drawn says, "Wonderful, you really captured our personalities in this work!" that comment can be seen as validation of the artist's (the action researcher's) work. If you as an action researcher ask the students in your class to react to the conclusions you have drawn on their work and they say, "Yep, that sure describes our work perfectly!" you can use that statement as a piece of data that supports your findings.

However, Lightfoot also makes the point that an artist is not required to adjust the portrait just because the client objects to it. If when asked for an opinion of the finished portrait the client says, "I don't like it. You make me look foolish," the artist is perfectly free to reply, "I'm sorry that you see yourself as a scholar, but I am the artist, and I see you as a fool. This picture should represent how I, the artist, see you."

In the example of Richard and Georgia's project, if they shared their findings with their students and asked what the students thought, they might hear the following comment:

> We agree completely. This was the most fun, most rewarding, and best work we've produced all year. Furthermore, we all plan to become more involved in our school, classrooms, and communities now that we've completed a RWAP!

Conversely, they might hear comments like the following:

> We disagree! This was too hard, took too long, and was boring. We hope we never have to do another project like this one!

If the majority of the class concurred with the first statement, then Richard and Georgia might be prepared to say:

> We are even more confident of our summary assertions now, because when we shared this information with the students and asked for their confidential responses, 92 percent of the students reported that our findings were on target.

If, however, the majority sentiment was similar to the negative comment, Georgia and Richard would face two options. They could, and perhaps should, reconsider their assertions. It would be appropriate for them to use the contrary opinion of the students as a cause to reassess their conclusions and consider whether they wanted to still stand behind them. It would also be perfectly acceptable for them to change their assertions at this point. If, upon further review, they wanted to stand behind their conclusions, they might say something like this:

> Although the majority (55 percent) of our students disagreed with our findings and told us that their hard work was based on the impact of this project on their final grades, not on the merits of the RWAP itself, we still stand behind our assertions. We do so because the reports from the other teachers and the reports from parents, coupled with our own observations and years of experience, lead us to believe that the positive changes were simply too profound to be accounted for by grade sanctions alone.

Revisiting the Graphic Reconstruction

At this point the analysis process is almost complete. Just one step remains: reviewing and perhaps revising your theory. Chapter 6 discussed the relationship between theory and action. The fundamental purpose of this type of teacher action research is to see if and in what ways our theories hold up in light of the data and in what ways, if any, our hunches or preliminary theories were in error.

Now is the time to consider your original theory and the way you understood it (as illustrated in your graphic reconstruction) and contrast it with the story that actually emerged from the data. Invariably, researchers find that their original theory needs some revision when examined in light of the data they collected. On rare occasions, an entire theory is proven wrong, or the data confirm that a theory is 100 percent correct. However, far more often, new data help refine our original theories into better and truer pictures of reality.

After reflecting on your original theory and your findings, it is time to once again take out the Post-it notes and a sheet of chart paper and draw another graphic reconstruction of your theory as you now understand it. (Follow the instructions for creating a graphic reconstruction in Chapter 6.)

The next chapter discusses how to report or share our learnings with other educators, students, and parents. One key aspect of that sharing is reporting on how our theoretical perspective has evolved as a consequence of data collection. Here again an analogy might help. Perhaps because I began my career as a social studies teacher, I have always found that visual depictions (maps) of our understandings tell a powerful story, particularly when viewed over time.

A very powerful history lesson could be taught by displaying on the classroom wall a set of four world maps: a map drawn before Columbus's first voyage, a map drawn after Magellan first circumnavigated the globe, a map dated 1950, and a map made through satellite imagery. By viewing these maps in sequence, students could derive significant insights into humankind's evolving understanding of the physical properties of our planet.

Similarly, if you save your graphic reconstructions regarding your evolving understandings about a critical issue of teaching and learning throughout your career, you will be assembling a chronological gallery of your enhanced understandings of your "world." There is no better testimony of your ever-increasing professional efficacy than this evidence of your growth as a professional educator. Looking back and seeing how you've grown as a result of what you've learned cannot help but reinforce the belief that you are a key player in an increasingly dynamic profession.

11 Putting the Action into Action Research

Laypeople are often curious about the work of "professional researchers." They, like many of us, find it hard to understand people who spend time watching others and theorizing, yet choose to not participate in the action themselves. The primary reason most of us entered teaching was not to make great discoveries about human learning, but rather to provide the best possible education for students. This brings us to the "So what?" question. Yes, it's nice to gain insights through research findings and to refine theories, but the big question for action researchers (the *actors* in this process) is, "What are we going to do differently now that we are equipped with all this new information?"

I've lost count of how many presentations of teacher research I've attended. But one thing I recall from every time I've witnessed educators reporting to other teachers on their classroom inquiries is the audience being intently interested in the researcher's action plans. This is probably no different from what occurs in other action-oriented fields. Although practicing physicians need to understand the basic biochemistry that affects their patients' health, what probably excites them more than anything else are the implications of research for practice. This may be even more true for teachers.

There is no one way to build an action plan. Planning for instruction is above all else a creative process. When faced with a choice from among a variety of plausible alternatives, making a judgment about what action will best fit individual teaching strengths, content, and students' characteristics requires artistry as well as knowledge. For the inquiring action researcher, a big part of the action planning process involves answering this question:

Given what I now know, what do I want to do or what do I think I should do differently?

Georgia and Richard found this process relatively easy. Because they were impressed with the quality of their students' work and the apparent changes in their students' perceptions of social efficacy, the next steps became readily apparent:

• Continue the Real World Advocacy Project (RWAP) assignment with all 8th grade civics students.
• Replicate this study next year to see if it works as well with a different group of students.
• Prepare all students for the RWAP as 7th graders with a short preliminary field experience.
• Add a requirement for periodic (weekly) debriefings with RWAP groups to keep projects from becoming overwhelming.
• Share the RWAP data with colleagues, get their feedback on implications for experiential problem-based learning, and forward their suggestions to the curriculum coordinating council.

Often the action planning process is as simple as it was for Richard and Georgia, especially when the research follows a *quasi-experimental* format, as theirs did. This is because quasi-experimental research is concerned with the testing of ideas (hypotheses). If the idea (hypothesis) works, the action researcher will want to find ways to implement it more often or more deeply. Alternatively, if the intervention was unsuccessful, it becomes equally clear that changes are in order (although the nature of those changes might not be so obvious). On the other hand, when the focus of the inquiry is *descriptive*—that is, the inquiry is intended to increase understanding of what is going on or to better illuminate a particular phenomenon—then the action planning process can become more complex. After completing a descriptive study, the action researcher might ask: *Now that I understand this phenomenon better, what theory/theories would I like to test?*

The answer to that question will be based upon the theoretical perspective (the most recent graphic reconstruction) the descriptive data helped produce. Occasionally a descriptive study will lead to another descriptive study. However, more often than not, once teacher researchers complete a descriptive study and consequently have a greater understanding of a phenomenon/issue, they become eager to try out an idea or two to improve the situation. This explains why descriptive studies are often precursors of later quasi-experimental studies.

Action Planning Steps

Whether your original research was descriptive or quasi-experimental, you might tackle the "what's next?" question in the same manner. Simply return to that part of the problem formulation process (discussed in Chapter 4) in which you explicated your theory for change. The action planning process follows steps that are very similar to the ones that gave rise to your initial research questions.

• Build a priority pie to answer the question: *Given what I know now, what are the most critical factors for me to address if I am to be more successful in this area?*

• Build a graphic reconstruction to answer the question: *What precisely do I think should be done to increase student/teacher success in this area?*

• Ask yourself: *Do any alternative theories/approaches have promise for addressing this problem?* If so, construct a graphic reconstruction to illustrate each of those approaches.

• List the pros and cons of each alternative theory.

• Analyze the pros and cons, and then, based upon that analysis, choose a plan of action.

Chapter 13 discusses "breakthrough technology," which is an action planning approach that works well when teams of researchers are working on schoolwide issues.

Reporting

There are probably as many different ways to report on action research as there are action researchers. What is so nice about this part of the process is that action researchers are liberated from the format restrictions that limit the creativity of traditional researchers. Conventional scientific research must be reported in writing, and the format for journal articles is usually proscribed in great detail. Teacher researchers are under no obligation to follow these constraints (unless they plan to use their classroom research as part of a degree program). As an action researcher your goals for reporting ought to be few and straightforward:

• You want other educators to hear, in your words, what you've learned.

• You want those hearing of your research to invest credibility in your findings.

• You want to hear the reaction of other professionals to the implications (the action plans) you developed.

An Executive Summary

First and foremost, you want to make your work accessible. To this end, your busy colleagues will appreciate it very much if you continue to perform in the role of executive secretary throughout the reporting phase. Not infrequently, researchers as well as executive secretaries prepare what are called executive summaries of larger works. The executive summary provides a reader with more detail than is usually found in an abstract, but it eliminates the need to wade through the entire piece of work.

Text and Appendix

It may be helpful to think of a research report as a seesaw. If on one side the text of the report is heavy, discussing in great detail the data that informed the study, then you need not include too much material as an appendix. This is because the text of the report contains everything necessary to establish credibility. The reverse is also true. If the text portion is abbreviated and discusses only the specific data that led to each conclusion, then balancing it with a comprehensive appendix is a good idea. An appendix that contains the raw data gives the consumers of the research an opportunity to reach their own conclusions (if they are willing to invest the time).

Illustrating the Story

There's truth in the old adage "A picture is worth a thousand words." Charts, graphs, and figures are effective ways to illustrate what you've learned from your data, and you should use them liberally as supplements to your written or spoken explanations.

Evaluating Audience Needs

When you go to a session at a conference or pick up a journal article, you generally approach the material with a motivation to learn more. Often a catchy title or a stimulating 25-word description is what has attracted your attention. For example:

> *Session 17b: An Exploration into the Development of Scientific Reasoning.* Two 6th grade teachers share the results of a two-year project to develop students' scientific reasoning through the use of multidisciplinary units.

You wouldn't be attending this session were it not for your interest in the topic. However, the program description only tells you so much. It has given you enough information to tell you that this is a session you might want to attend, but not much more.

When I go to a session, I approach the material through a "hierarchy of needs." Until my lower-level needs are met, it is hard to be receptive or even focus on the information presented. I see the audience members' hierarchy of needs as a set of questions that must be answered in sequence:

1. Who are you and where are you coming from?

It is unlikely that any audience for your action research works in a context identical to your own. Schools and individual classrooms differ by level, size, funding, student demographics, and so on. Don't be concerned, as it is unlikely that anyone would lose interest in your research simply because you teach in a different setting. However, they will come to your session with a built-in need to know which filters to put on to help them translate, interpret, and understand your story. Just because research was done in an affluent suburb doesn't mean that it won't have lessons for an inner-city audience, but the audience won't know how to interpret your findings unless they are made aware of your context. This is why it is essential that at the outset of an action research presentation you (and your colleagues, if working as a team) share the following information:

• Who you are, why you are interested in this topic, and what the relationship is among the researchers, as well as the individual responsibilities of each team member in conducting the research.

• The nature of the setting where the research was conducted: for example, the type of community the school serves, the most prevalent characteristics of the students, the staff's perception of the greatest needs of the students.

• Significant factors about the school such as its level, size, adequacy of funding, and history of innovation.

2. What are your judgments based upon? What types of data did you collect?

The answer to this question is the action researcher's equivalent of the "methodology" section of the traditional lab report. If you neglect this part, even though the audience may understand where you are "coming from," they may not know whether they should invest any confidence in your conclusions. It is not necessary to fill the air with a string of mind-numbing polysyllabic terms to describe your method of statistical analysis, but it is essential that you tell the audience how you learned what you did and why they should consider the data to be valid and reliable.

After providing the answers to these two questions, it's time to present your data collection matrix. You should share the details and rationale for each of the specific techniques included in your triangulated data collection plan and explain why you believed these data would ultimately create a valid and reliable picture of the phenomenon you studied. Specifically,

• List each question that guided the research and the data collection techniques you used to answer that question.
• Explain how you analyzed your data and drew your conclusions.

3. What did you learn? Why did you reach these particular conclusions?

This begins the most exciting and important aspect of any action research report. In short, this is a major reason why teaching colleagues would invest the time to hear about your inquiry. They want to piggyback on your experience and learn what you learned (without having to spend the time learning for themselves). This is why you should allocate substantial time for this portion of your presentation. This is where summary charts and graphs come in. Drawing someone's attention to a conclusion (for example, that student achievement went up) without first sharing the way you determined "achievement" will confuse your audience. That is why you should share scoring guides and the basis for your evaluations in answer to question 2.

Here's a list of suggested items to include when presenting your conclusions:

• A comprehensive list of findings
• A list of assertions
• Questions that you feel still need to be answered
• The theoretical perspective you now hold based on these findings (your updated graphic reconstruction)

4. What you are planning to do now? Should other teachers pursue that direction based upon your findings?

In my experience, if the first three needs (questions 1 through 3) are adequately addressed, the report moves into high gear when presenters come to question 4. In fact, if the work is being presented at a conference, it is at this point that the presentation often evolves into a spirited dialogue between researcher and audience. All teachers are driven by one overriding question: *What can I do that will make a difference for my kids?* This final piece (the action plan) of an action research report presents the researcher's answer to that question in such a manner that it can be pondered, considered, debated, and questioned by others.

This concludes the description of the seven-step action research process. However, before we can consider our review of the action research process complete, it is wise to reflect on some of the ethical issues surrounding classroom research. Chapter 12 addresses several key ethical and methodological issues.

12 Methodological and Ethical Issues

At this point many of you may be asking, "All this sounds fine for the teachers, but how will parents react when they hear we are experimenting with their children?" This important question needs to be squarely addressed. Answering it involves an examination of two intertwined issues: research methodology and the ethical obligations of teacher researchers. Let's begin by considering a largely methodological question that has significant ethical overtones:

> *Is it appropriate for teachers to use experimental methods with their students?*

Experimental Designs

You may wonder, "When is it proper to use students as guinea pigs?" That sounds like an appropriate question, particularly because throughout this text I have framed action research as a quasi-experimental science. However, I would argue that this question arises only when teacher research is viewed through the wrong lens.

Teaching is above all a sacred responsibility—a calling that is governed by licensure, professional ethics, and codes of professional conduct. Fundamentally, each of these ethical codes demands that teachers as professionals continuously provide each student with the best learning experiences that they know how to deliver. To deny any child access to a quality educational practice for any reason is not only abrogating their professional duty, but places that child at a disadvantage. No concern for scientific precision or research methodology should ever take precedence over the obligation to provide each child with the best possible teaching.

The "guinea pig" issue arises most often when action researchers believe that the only way to determine the quality of an innovative practice is through the use of an experimental design complete with treatment and control groups. The premise of the treatment-control paradigm is that if researchers study two identical groups, differing only in a single variable (the one being tested), then any changes observed must have been "caused" by the independent variable.

Even though such an approach may sound great, it is, in fact, impossible to carry out. No one could control for all relevant variables when dealing with human beings in social situations. Worse yet, the very act of assigning a student to a control group when the researcher believes that the treatment provided to the other students is superior is to deny the control students the "best possible instruction." That is far too high a price to pay for a clean piece of research.

However, even if researchers were equally impressed with two approaches, unless they raised their students in cages like laboratory rats, they would never be able to say that they had controlled every meaningful distinction between two students or groups of students. For these and many other reasons, educators should be extremely skeptical of any researcher who claims to have "proven causality."

What teacher researchers *can* demonstrate to support their assertions are strong *correlations*. When the goal is to produce evidence of strong correlations, control groups aren't always necessary. Being incapable of proving causation shouldn't be disappointing. Daily life frequently involves taking action based not on causality but on correlates. Here's an example of how a teacher might assert a correlation that leads to action:

> When we did x and y with this group of students, z resulted. Because we wanted to see the students become proficient at z and because consistently we saw proficiency with z following our work on x and y, we plan to continue x and y exactly as we have before.

There are a number of valid and reliable ways to produce data showing the correlation and association between the instruction provided and the performance of students. Using these methods can effectively eliminate a need to use the treatment-control paradigm.

Comparative Case Studies

Occasionally the goal of research is to resolve disputes over competing pedagogical approaches. In such circumstances an excellent strategy is using what is called a *cross-case analysis*.

How should a school arbitrate conflicts when and if they occur regarding alternative approaches to accomplishing an instructional objective? These issues arise frequently in schools and often result in divisiveness. The political resolution of pedagogical issues produces groups of winners and losers, often followed by a rapidly deteriorating school climate. In recent years, schools all across North America have experienced intraschool civil wars over questions involving such issues as the best way to teach reading, varied approaches to discipline, and alternative approaches to achieving math literacy. Faculties often find themselves in deep conflict over such issues as well as over which instructional materials or methods to adopt.

The most common approach to resolving these conflicts is using what I have called *bias-based decision making* (Sagor, 1996); others mistakenly call it democracy. This occurs most often after everyone has been invited to take a look at the materials or listen to the arguments made by those advocating for each side. Teachers are then asked to vote for their favorite. The district or school declares the winner to be the "best available method." Later it is adopted and the students of a school are left without any choice but to experience the adopted program. The minority of the faculty that voted for the other approach is then denied any chance to use or to further explore what they may still believe are the "best available practices."

When the work of a study group (see Chapter 13) reveals that competing or compelling alternative approaches exist, each with real promise for meeting students' needs, a productive strategy for a school is to commission alternative pilot projects. This happens frequently in cases involving the adoption of textbooks and other materials. For example, it is not at all uncommon for teachers to be asked to try out different materials for a finite period of time to determine whether one approach is easier to use or is more beneficial for the students. This raises a good question: Why are "clinical trials" in education always so short lived? Do we really believe that all the critical questions of teaching and learning can be resolved in short six-week trials?

Feigning Certainty

Many school administrators fear that extended pilot projects or field trials would undermine public confidence in the schools. They couldn't be more wrong! The habit of *feigning certainty*, taking the position that one particular method is the answer for all students, probably fosters more suspicion about competence than would an open admission of uncertainty.

Research in advertising has shown that when salespeople act too sure of themselves, it appears they are trying to fool people. The same phenomenon happens in schools. Parents are given choices by all the other professionals with whom they interact. The architect who designs a home offers each client choices in style, materials, allocation of space, and other design considerations; likewise the lawyer offers alternative means to solve a legal dilemma; and the doctor suggests alternative treatment regimes for the patient's consideration. So why do educational leaders feel the need to isolate and deliver the "one and only" answer to every learning problem?

This habit of arguing that there is one simple answer to every complex question has resulted in the heated pedagogical wars being waged across the land. The public's angry reaction to the feigning of certainty is apparent in legislative efforts to overturn school practices such as bilingual education, family life education, and character education and to provide for greater parental choice. What are the alternatives to feigning certainty? When a school finds itself genuinely divided over the merits of competing approaches, there's no need to rush to judgment. Instead, school leaders can frame the conflict as an opportunity rather than a problem. For example, they might consider declaring something like the following:

> Apparently we have a difference of professional opinion over the best ways to teach reading. This provides us with a wonderful opportunity to test the merits of alternative approaches with our students in the context of our curriculum and in light of our goals. What we learn could be a real help for us as we endeavor to provide our students with the very best possible educational opportunities.

The school leadership could then solicit alternative proposals for pilot projects. A good way to institutionalize this is with a policy such as the following:

> Proposals for pilot projects will be approved providing the project is consistent with our goals and will not cost substantially more than other alternatives under consideration. To be considered, a proposal must be based on sound theory, and a commitment must be made to conduct a viable assessment using previously agreed upon criteria and a willingness to report the results to the school community.

To understand how this might work and to see how it provides a viable alternative to the treatment/control methodology, let's look at how an elementary school in Washington State worked on the issue of grouping for developmentally appropriate instruction.

Multiple Pilot Projects in Practice

The faculty at Scenic Beach Elementary School[1] was united in its philosophy that children are best served in a developmentally appropriate setting. Furthermore, the teachers at Scenic Beach were committed to providing coverage of the adopted district curriculum and to preparing their children for success with the state's required essential learnings. What they disagreed about was the best method by which to achieve those goals. Following intense study, three teams of teachers (two primary teams and an intermediate team) found themselves attracted to the idea that team-taught, multi-aged classrooms offered the better way to provide a developmentally appropriate learning environment. The other 20 teachers perceived things differently. They believed that single-teacher, single-level, and single-age classrooms provided the preferable learning environment.

Because the norm at Scenic Beach was the single-teacher, single-level, single-age class and the concept of team-taught, multi-aged classes was the departure, the principal solicited a proposal from the teachers who wanted to pursue the multi-age model. Implicitly, the principal followed a policy like the one presented earlier. After visiting schools using the multi-age model, attending professional conferences focused on this approach, and spending dozens of hours in collegial discourse, the teachers prepared a proposal for multi-age education. It was well thought through and theoretically grounded. At this point, interested parents were invited to come to the school to hear more about this proposal for an innovative pilot project.

At well-attended evening meetings, parents heard from the teachers about the perceived benefits of this alternative approach to grouping. Equally important, parents were encouraged to raise questions and concerns they might have regarding the proposed pilot project. After the informational meetings, parents were given a choice of having their children placed in the team-taught classes or the traditional configurations. The following school year began with no individuals (students, teachers, or parents) captive to an approach that made them uncomfort-

---

[1]Scenic Beach is a pseudonym. This study was reported in Wagner (1997).

able. As is often the case when parents are given these types of choices, it wasn't difficult for the principal to satisfy everyone; although a number of parents expressed a preference for one of the alternatives, an even larger number were open to either approach, simply deferring to the judgment of the staff on which approach was best for their child. The process of giving parents and students a choice of treatments is an excellent alternative to using assigned treatment/control groups.

Other Alternatives to Control Groups

As mentioned earlier, the purpose of the control group in experimental science is to provide a clear contrast to the performance of those subjects experiencing an intervention. Because it is nearly impossible to prove causality in educational settings, we must instead look for strong, positive correlations between treatments and outcomes. As researchers, we need to demonstrate that the performance of students, when using a particular approach, is superior to what those same students would likely have achieved were it not for the intervention being investigated. Listed below are three ways to accomplish this without denying any child the services that we or the students' parents believe they deserve:

- Compare "treatment" students' performance to their own previous performance.
- Compare "treatment" students to students taught in previous years by the same teacher using a different method.
- Compare "treatment" students to students in another teacher's class.

Comparing Students to Themselves

Figure 12.1 is a graph that depicts the math scores of a group of 6th grade students at the time their teacher was implementing an innovative math program.

The question before this teacher researcher might be: Was this the type of growth that I would normally have expected from these students had I not used the innovative program? One way to answer that question would be to look at the past performance of these same students. After collecting this information, the teacher could plot earlier "rates of growth" on the same type of graph. Figure 12.2 shows the pattern of growth for these same students in math during the previous three years.

When these two trend lines are placed on the same graph and the line representing earlier performance is extended at the same slope (see

FIGURE 12.1
Change in Math Scores from 5th Grade to 6th Grade

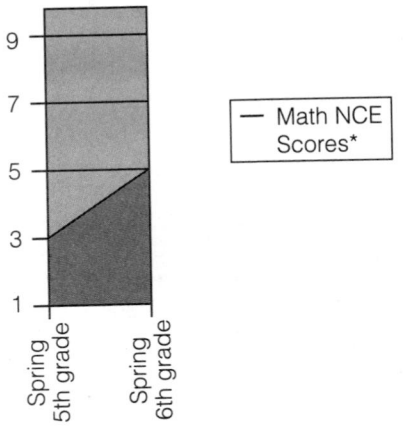

*Performance is reported using "normal curve equivalence" (NCE), indicated by the scores shown along the left side of the figure. The NCE is a good way to track the rate of growth from one year to the next.

FIGURE 12.2
Math Scores During Previous Three Years

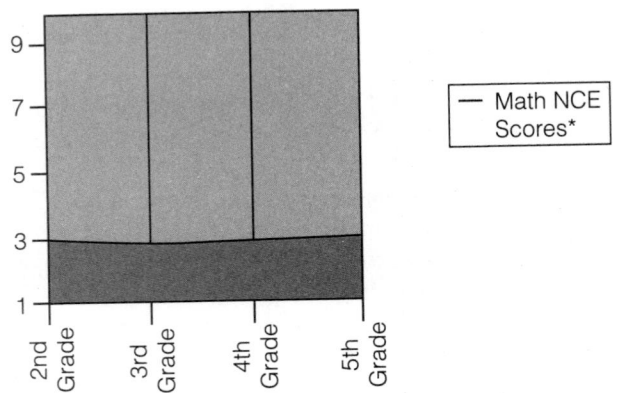

*Performance is reported using "normal curve equivalence" (NCE), indicated by the scores shown along the left side of the figure. The NCE is a good way to track the rate of growth from one year to the next.

Figure 12.3), an observer could fairly infer that the difference between points *a* and *b* is a difference in performance that might be attributed to the program being researched.

Comparing Students to Other Students Taught by the Researcher

This strategy rests upon the assumption that if you had similar students both years and if the only substantial difference in your teaching was the innovation, then you might attribute differences in performance to the new wrinkle added to your instructional program. That conclusion, however, is based largely on the two "ifs." Specifically, if the two groups of students were substantially different, the comparison you are making would be between apples and oranges. Likewise, if you made major changes in your teaching methods beyond the introduction of the new program, differences observed in performance might just as easily be attributed to those other changes.

To minimize these problems, you must collect data on both of these contextual issues (past and present student characteristics and past and present teaching practices) and present them whenever you share your

FIGURE 12.3

Predicted vs. Actual Pattern of Improvement in Math Scores

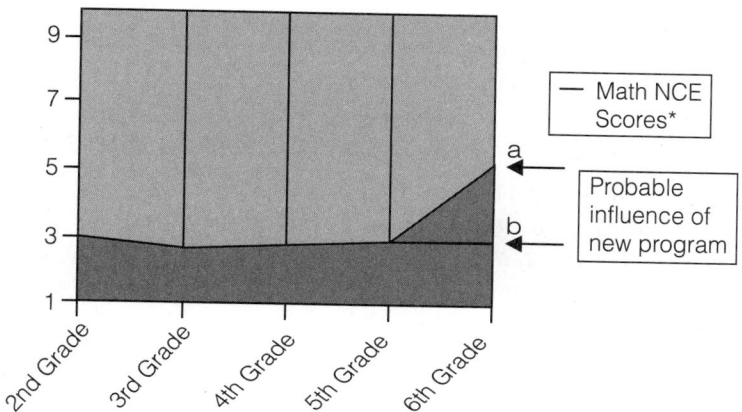

*Performance is reported using "normal curve equivalence" (NCE), indicated by the scores shown along the left side of the figure. The NCE is a good way to track the rate of growth from one year to the next.

research. This need not be difficult. To compare student groups, collect information on relevant demographic characteristics, such as

- Gender
- Ethnicity
- Past performance and grades
- Past achievement levels on standardized tests
- Behavior and attendance patterns

If the profiles of this year's and last year's students are nearly identical on the above key demographic dimensions, then comparing the groups would likely be appropriate. If they are not, then you should consider a slightly different option, the stratified sample. This involves comparing the treatment group to a subset of the previous year's students (selected in a manner that matches the treatment group's demographics). On occasion the groups are significantly different across most dimensions, and it is not possible to pull a comparison group that matches the treatment group. When that occurs, you simply need to alert consumers of the research to all the important differences between the groups. A statement like the following could well suffice:

> Figure x illustrates the difference in performance in math of my 6th grade students this year compared to the students who were in my 6th grade class last year. However, it should be pointed out that last year's class had significantly more girls (20) than did this year's group (10), as well as 6 students with significant behavior problems (defined as three or more office referrals per semester). Although the superior performance of this year's students may have been influenced by the new math program, it could also have been influenced by these differences in gender or the presence of the disruptive students in last year's class.

Comparing Students to Another Teacher's Students

A third strategy calls for finding another class or school that serves demographically similar students and uses a program similar to the one you are using. However, such comparisons are also based upon two assumptions about the groups:

- The students are largely alike.
- The most significant difference between the groups is the instructional approach being studied.

If you can support those assumptions, then it is fair to infer that changes or differences in performance are likely associated with the intervention. As with all of these approaches, you will enhance an audience's confidence in your conclusions by using triangulation (multiple independent sources of data on the impact of the intervention).

Research Without a Control Group

The previous discussion is based upon an assumption that to produce high-quality research, a researcher must have a comparison group. This simply isn't so. We can evaluate and enjoy a piece of artwork without comparing it to another work. It would even sound silly to say, "This Van Gogh is 40 percent better than that Matisse." In our daily lives we constantly make judgments that we are quite confident about regarding the goodness of artwork, friends, communities, clubs, churches, and so forth, without feeling a need for a group to statistically compare them to. We do this by deliberately examining the object of study across criteria that are deemed important. We then make a judgment on the object's "intrinsic" goodness, not about its "relative" goodness.

For example, in friends, I value many factors, including loyalty, caring, listening ability, a fun-loving nature, and spontaneity. When I have gathered evidence over the years that a person has all those traits, I declare they are a treasured friend, I don't need to quantify it with a number or a comparison. Similarly, a vacation is a good experience if it meets the implicit criteria of our family for a good time. We might (for fun) rank our favorite vacations, but we don't need to create a graph to prove if we had 10 percent more or less fun than in past years. In many cases, it is possible to appreciate important things without the need for a comparison group.

Qualitative Research

Thus far we have explored issues related to research questions that emerge from conflicting perspectives on a problem and that are initiated to help shed light on the merits of one approach over another—for example, multi-age grouping versus grade-level grouping, or one year's teaching method compared with the previous year's teaching method. To answer these types of questions, researchers usually employ one of the "quasi-experimental" methodologies discussed earlier. Quasi-experimental research is valuable and helpful to test a hypothesis. However, often research questions don't involve hypotheses, but rather they grow from a desire to develop deeper understanding of a phenomenon—to shed light on an issue and to be able to describe it in a way that ultimately will lead to greater insights. This type of research is descriptive in nature and is often called "qualitative" research. It is so called because it seeks to describe and illuminate the qualities that are present in phenomena rather than to rank, number, or otherwise assess them.

Educators don't often admit how much they depend on qualitative data to help inform policy as well as day-to-day decisions. For this reason, a few examples of how qualitative data influences policy would prove helpful here.

In recent years few policy issues have concerned classroom teachers more than finding the best learning environments and placements for those students who bring unique challenges to their education. I recall two action research projects conducted by teachers at Eleanor Roosevelt Elementary School (Sagor, 1995) in Vancouver, Washington, that proved extremely helpful and productive for that faculty in dealing with special education policy issues. Both studies were qualitative, or descriptive, in nature.

Hollis Burt was a kindergarten teacher who was also certified in special education. She and her colleagues were wondering whether inclusion or resource room programs were the best intervention for young children with disabilities. A related issue was whether full-day or half-day programs were best for those young children with identified learning problems. To answer these questions, she undertook a qualitative cross-case study. Watching four children over the course of a year, each with a different program (full- and half-day, inclusion and resource room), Hollis thoroughly documented the experiences of these children, including the individual education plan objectives they accomplished and the reactions of their parents and teachers. Her report made the experience of these kids come to life. She did not choose to use an experimental design for her study because, in her opinion, each of the four children she was studying was far too unique in learning attributes to be compared with anyone else.

Interestingly, all four of the children flourished. It was apparent that each child was being educated in the correct manner for that child. This descriptive study helped the Roosevelt faculty realize that it would be a mistake to prescribe any one program format for all kindergartners with disabilities. They were quite comfortable making that decision after looking at four well-documented qualitative case studies.

Jeannette Whiting, a teacher of a multi-age class for 8- to 10-year-olds at Roosevelt, decided to explore another issue related to inclusion by studying, in depth, the experience of one multiply handicapped child included in her classroom. Ashley (a pseudonym) had cerebral palsy, and for the first time in her school career she was participating in a mainstream class. Jeannette wanted to know how well this option served Ashley, how it was affecting the other children in her class, and how it was affecting her teaching. In the end, Jeannette found that Ashley had a very good year; she gained a great deal socially and academically from the inclusion experience, as did her classmates. Furthermore, her presence in the class was a source of growth and satisfaction for Jeannette.

What I recall most from later watching Jeannette's presentation of her research to teacher groups is the rapt attention that it received from the audience. The deep teacher interest in this piece of descriptive research helped me learn a powerful lesson regarding qualitative research and the issue of drawing general conclusions.

One misconception that many educators have about research is that it is only helpful when it is "generalizable." Generalizability refers to the degree to which findings of a study can be applied to and transferred to another contextually different setting. For example, the finding that water freezes at 32 degrees Fahrenheit at sea level is generalizable. Go any place on earth, stand at sea level, cool water to a temperature of 32 degrees, and it will freeze. Often when researchers contend that something worked at their school, people who desire generalizability will ask, "Does this mean it will work in our school?" In most cases the answer should be no, because our action research is usually conducted in a unique setting with a comparatively small sample (for example, one classroom, one school). However, this shouldn't diminish anyone's enthusiasm for small-scale action research. Those who say ungeneralizable research isn't valuable to educators are just plain wrong!

If teachers valued only generalizable research, they would have no interest in research like Jeannette's. After all, no two students with disabilities are ever identical, and it is a fair guess that no other teacher in her school would ever encounter another child with characteristics identical to Ashley's. In addition, no other teacher in the school had a history, temperament, or teaching style identical to Jeannette's. Furthermore, the chemistry of each classroom is different, based upon the unique composition of each class. For these reasons the findings in Jeannette's study couldn't possibly be said to be generalizable.

So why have I seen dozens of teachers voluntarily attending her presentations and listening with such rapt attention to her study? I believe it is because they were hearing a valid and reliable report of what occurred inside one unique setting. Furthermore, as intellectual beings themselves, these other teachers were quite capable of drawing their own conclusions about what relevance this single case report might have for them, their teaching, and their classes.

It is a myth that all good science is made up of generalizable findings. In fact, much of science, particularly social science but also medicine, geology, and other natural sciences, is built upon case-by-case studies that offer valid and reliable reports about unique situations. The consumers of this type of research—thinking scientists and practitioners like you and me—are then free to extrapolate if and when we think it fits our particular situation, clients, classes, or school.

Informed Consent

The question raised at the start of this chapter, "When is it appropriate to treat kids like guinea pigs?" has one fundamental answer: *never*. It is our sacred obligation as educators to give each child the best, most empowering education we possibly can every day. Experimenting on students should not be what education is about.

You might be asking how I dare make such a statement when this book has made many references to teaching as an "experimental" science and the use of "quasi-experimental" methods. I feel comfortable answering with the following logic: The subjects of our research are ourselves. We are in the business of learning how to become the best teachers we possibly can be. To do so we are testing how effective we can become. Every day that I teach I am experimenting—experimenting on myself, seeing what works with and for me. Yes, the students are intimately involved in the process. But I try to keep in mind two parameters regarding their involvement in my research:

• They are receiving the best possible instruction I know how to deliver. I am not doing nor providing anything different for or to a child than I would be doing were I not involved in teacher research.

• Although they are not the subjects of my experiment (I am), they are critical sources of data on my teaching effectiveness.

The professional research community is held to high ethical standards. The most important of these is the requirement of receiving "informed consent" from anyone who will be the subject of a study. In the case of subjects under the age of majority, a parent or guardian must grant this consent. The purpose of this is to ensure that no one is ever unknowingly subjected to any form of harm without having the risks clearly explained in advance.

I think we should, and could, argue that the students in our classes are more like data unearthed by historians and used to explain historical phenomena than subjects being manipulated for the sole purpose of an experiment. They are simply and naturally living through our instruction (the same instruction they would have been receiving had we never even heard of action research), and we, like historians, are curious as to what it was like living through this small bit of history.

That notwithstanding, I have come to believe that it is prudent to obtain permission, whether legally needed or not, for these reasons:

• If you elect, after conducting your research, to use student work, pictures, or comments in reports of your research outside the school setting (permission isn't needed to discuss students with other colleagues in your school), you will need to secure parental permission first. This is because their words, work, and ideas are their property alone.

• Given the scrutiny that public education is under, erring on the side of prudence in areas that concern student and parent rights is, in my opinion, well worth it.

Based on the above parameters and rationale, I suggest that teacher researchers send a permission request to all parents at the outset of each school year. The generic letter (shown in Figure 12.4) was developed to convey the following points:

• I'm conducting this research for myself.
• The benefit your child will receive is a better teacher.
• The research will not mean that different things will happen to your child. Nothing will be granted or denied due to the research.
• With your permission, I might use your child's work, words, or ideas.
• There will be no negative consequences for your child if permission is denied. I simply won't use his/her work, words, or ideas in my research.

The greatest risk from asking for permission is that some parents will deny it and you will have only 25 students whose work you can report on as opposed to 30. The benefits that you will receive—respect from parents for your effort to consistently improve your teaching and the protection from a charge of unethical behavior—make it a step well worth taking.

FIGURE 12.4

Request for Permission

Dear Parent,

This year I will be conducting some research on my own teaching. I am doing this so that I can continue to refine my practice and provide my students with the best possible teaching.

I would like to use the work produced by my students this year as data for my research and would, therefore, like your permission to use your child's opinions/work in my study.

I assure you confidentiality will be maintained and your child will not be identified by me in any way. In addition, your child will not be denied any instruction or benefits because of my inquiry.

If I have your permission to use _____[child's name]_____ work in my research, please return this form with your approval.

Sincerely,

Dick Sagor

I grant my permission for the use of _____[child's full name]_____
ideas, schoolwork, or words in research conducted during this school year by her teacher, Richard Sagor. I understand that every good faith effort will be made to maintain confidentiality in any reports of this research. I understand that if I do not grant this permission, he/she will not be denied any educational opportunity.

_____   _____
Parent/Guardian   Date

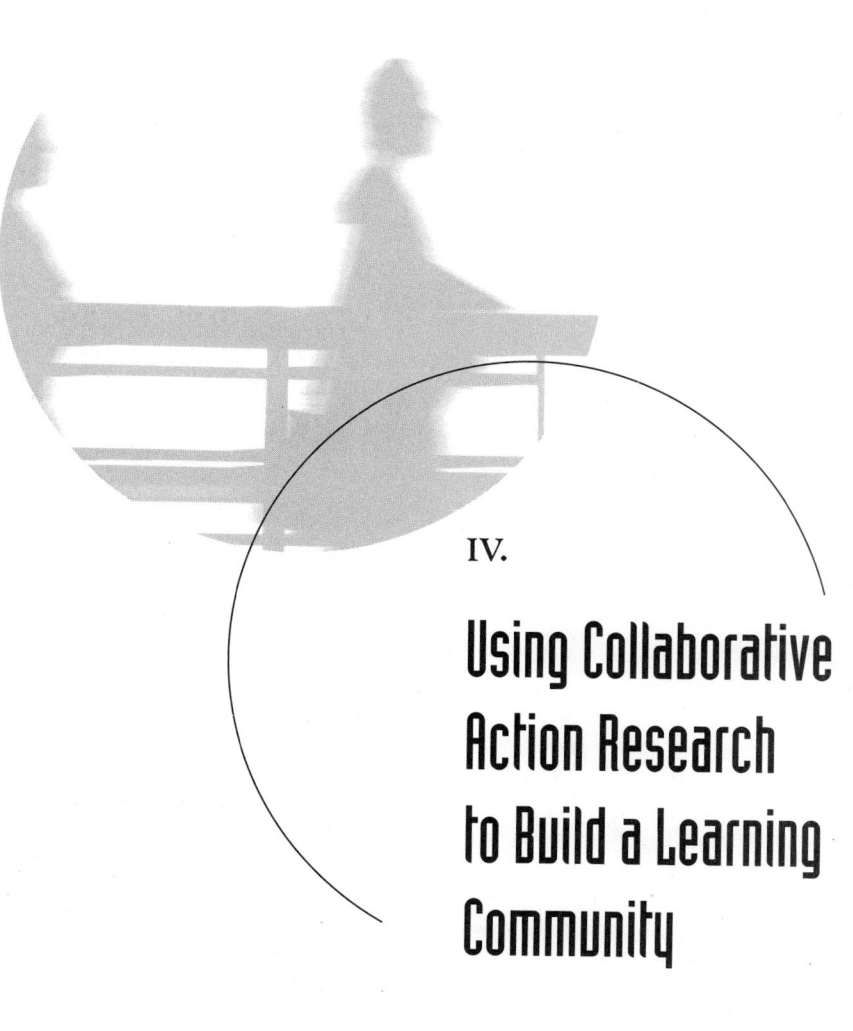

IV.

Using Collaborative
Action Research
to Build a Learning
Community

13 Collaborative Action Research and School Culture

The most exciting moment of my professional career was when I first heard the late Ron Edmonds speak. As he shared his then ground-breaking research on effective schools, I heard empirical confirmation of my belief that schools are capable of preparing all students for equality of opportunity.

The work of Edmonds (1979), Brookover and Lezotte (1979), Rutter, Maughn, Mortimore, Ouston, and Smith (1979), and the other effective schooling researchers who followed in their footsteps provided all the positive proof needed to establish that schools do indeed make the critical difference in student learning, that nurture is more powerful than nature, and that school characteristics are better predictors of student performance than socioeconomic status. This was the most exciting piece of social research I could ever have imagined. To realize that educators had in their power the means to provide every child, regardless of social class, an equal opportunity to develop the academic skills necessary for lifelong success was all the vindication I needed for my decision to spend my life pursuing social justice through education.

That exhilaration was soon followed by years of frustration over the inability to clone effective schools. It appeared that the transformation of an ineffective school into an effective one required more than a focus on adopting a list of correlates. Fortunately, the findings of a new generation of researchers such as Sarason (1982), Schein (1992), Bryk and Driscoll (1988), Little (1982), and Rosenholtz (1989) helped illuminate the hidden ingredient of effectiveness—the mortar that binds the building blocks of effectiveness and the key factor that had apparently escaped the attention of the original effective school researchers. These researchers uncovered the power of *organizational culture*. They documented the reality that if educators work in environments that are true "communities of learners"—places that support professionalism, collaboration and inquiry—then improved student achievement would inevitably follow.

At first the implications of these findings seemed a bit peculiar to me. It isn't overstating this research to summarize it as saying that we could predict the direction of student performance in a school merely by observing the professional interactions of the school's staff. To me, this sounded counterintuitive. I assumed that if I wanted to know how good a school was, the most important thing would be to observe the work of the children. I wondered why the working conditions of the faculty should be so important. In trying to make sense of this finding, I sought a helpful analogy. Again, I found one in medicine.

I imagined being in a strange city and suffering from a mysterious affliction. I pondered how, if given the choice of being treated at one of two medical centers that I knew little about, I would make my choice. In my imaginary scenario, I was told that the doctors at the first medical center were nationally renowned for their expertise; however, because of their overpowering egos, they rarely collaborated or assisted one another other in any meaningful way. They tended to hoard their patients, rarely asked for second opinions, avoided referrals, and kept their innovative techniques to themselves as though they were closely guarded patents. The physicians at the other medical center didn't have prestigious international reputations; however, they worked in an atmosphere of intense collaboration. They regularly conferred on perplexing cases, assisted one another with procedures, and tutored each other on new techniques on an ongoing basis. Faced with choosing a venue for treatment, the decision would be easy for me. I'd go to the second medical center. It would seem to me that if I were receiving treatment from a staff that shared responsibility for my care, I would be placing myself in a far better position to receive the attention I needed than in a place where only one individual, regardless of how renowned, claimed to have all the answers.

Peter Senge (1990), in his landmark book *The Fifth Discipline: The Art and Science of the Learning Organization*, described the learning organization as a place where the culture supported

- Personal mastery
- Mental modeling
- Shared visions
- Team learning

Although all of these attributes contribute to a school's behavior as a learning organization, we will begin this discussion by looking at how action research can help a faculty develop the "discipline" of shared vision.

Collective Autonomy and Shared Vision

Carl Glickman (1993) has used the term *collective autonomy* to describe the way teachers behave in collegial school cultures. Although it sounds like an oxymoron, it captures the very essence of a professional educational environment.

As used by Glickman, the term *collective* refers to the commitment of a school's staff to develop and pursue a shared vision. All members of the school community enter into this commitment voluntarily. This is of no small consequence. Based upon my own research and experience with effective schools, I have come to believe that there is no place in the schoolhouse for someone electing to stand against the school's shared vision for student learning. I am not saying that holding a divergent vision from the prevailing one makes someone a less virtuous educator. On the contrary, the very process of having different schools pursuing different visions is what allows alternative perspectives on teaching and learning to be developed, demonstrated, and researched.

Nevertheless, the ultimate success of any organization is predicated upon an agreement of all key players to pull in the same direction. People who want to sell athletic shoes may be outstanding salespersons, but they will find little professional fulfillment in a consumer electronics store. Likewise, if a school is committed to enhancing the literacy of its students, a staff member who feels that language proficiency shouldn't be a priority will in the long (and short) run be happier and more productive working elsewhere.

The term *autonomy*, as used by Glickman, refers to the means employed by the members of the school community to make the school's collective vision come to life. Once again, an analogy from medicine may help.

Two partners in a cardiology practice might hold precisely the same (collective) vision for their patients—long, vital, healthy, lives—yet they could well find themselves in significant disagreement regarding the best treatment protocol to accomplish this. This is not necessarily bad. In fact, it is considered quite appropriate in the medical context. If one doctor reasons that following one theory of cardiac care will better achieve the goal of long-lived healthy patients, she will follow that theory. Meanwhile, her partner, believing an alternative therapy has more promise, will use the alternative approach. Ultimately, the clinic's patients will be the beneficiaries of this diversity. When dedicated health care professionals attempt alternative treatments, collect data on the efficacy of those treatments, and share what they have learned, then the entire clinic "learns itself forward." Ultimately, longitudinal data on patient progress will help these clinicians better understand which treatments are more effective for which patients. Most importantly, it will contribute to helping the larger enterprise (the medical profession) get closer to unraveling the riddle of heart disease.

Generating a Shared Vision

Vision is a term that has been overused and widely abused by school leaders. A cynical teacher might not be far off defining it this way: "Vision is a seven-word phrase placed on the top of district letterhead as the result of a $100,000 strategic planning initiative led by an outside consultant." A phrase such as "Helping build competent students for the 21st century" may be what some educators call vision, but it is a far cry from what Peter Senge and the cognitive psychologists who have conducted research on visualization have in mind when they employ the term.

To be productive, a vision has to convey a vivid portrait of an outcome in enough detail so that anyone who reads it or hears it can close his or her eyes and see precisely the same thing. This is what an author accomplishes when writing a successful piece of fiction. Although the protagonist in a novel might not actually exist, every reader of the novel has a similar vision of not only the character's appearance, but the very nature of the character's personality. Visions drawn by a good novelist are so effective that readers are even able to predict (with high interrater reliability) how the characters will react in future chapters.

A good way for educators to understand the vision-building process is by looking at the way high-technology companies use visioning in the development of their innovative products. They begin by producing a prototype, a mock-up that resembles what the finished product should look like. With this model in mind, it then becomes possible for dozens (sometimes hundreds) of engineers, often working thousands of miles apart, to achieve the required breakthroughs, to fabricate the components, to put the various pieces together, and to finally develop a product that fits the original vision.

Shared school visions serve similar purposes. If all members of a school community are able to close their eyes and visualize students achieving the same outcomes, then it becomes possible for them to work (sometimes in idiosyncratic ways and in separate departments, classrooms, or grade levels) toward the realization of the components of that shared vision. Of course, in some ways it is easier for people in business to achieve their vision. A major difference between educators and high-technology companies is that a high-technology company's visions are built with metal, silicon, and plastic, while educators' visions are usually contained in words and stories. In the book *Local Control and Accountability: How to Get It, Keep It, and Improve School Performance* (Sagor, 1996), I describe a process that many school faculties have found helpful when creating a shared vision. The process begins with each member of the school community engaging in reflective writing in response to the prompt shown in Figure 13.1 (p. 169).

Once all stakeholders have had a chance to write and reflect on what they see as concrete manifestations of school success, the scenarios are shared, modified, combined, and massaged until a single compelling story emerges that captures the shared dreams of the school community.

Figure 13.2 (pp. 170–171) is an abbreviated version of one school's shared vision of a successful student and the educational programs that they built to assist him in becoming a success. This scenario emerged from schoolwide deliberations at Almeria Middle School in Fontana, California. Almeria is a public school serving a diverse and economically disadvantaged community. At Almeria the visioning process preceded a major multiyear school restructuring campaign. The faculty found that once they agreed on what they wanted to achieve, all of them, regardless of their individual assignment, were able to explain in detail how their work (the means) contributed to the school's collective vision (the ends).

After authoring the composite vision, the next step for a school faculty is to examine the vision and tease out the critical components that contribute to the whole. A school staff might ask themselves at this juncture:

Considering our vision, what are the critical elements (processes and outcomes) that we believe are necessary to the development of this student?

The faculty at Almeria answered this question by identifying a list of targets (some were student achievement targets and others were program targets) and then indexing them as footnotes in the scenario document. These targets are listed in Figure 13.3 (p. 173).

Occasionally an entire faculty is of one mind regarding the best mechanism or strategies to achieve each element of their shared vision. However, that isn't always the case, nor should it be the norm. As in the example of the cardiology practice discussed earlier, valuable insights can often be garnered from the pursuit of alternative approaches. Necessity may be the mother of invention, but the testing of competing hypotheses is the mother of wisdom.

Breakthrough Technology

Once a school's faculty "owns" a shared vision, it is time to invite the faculty to be creative in making the breakthroughs necessary for achieving each of the components of the vision. Schools that have succeeded in becoming learning communities do this in the same manner that high-technology companies do.

When a computer software or hardware company decides it would be in its best interest to bring to market a product that is substantially different from those currently in the marketplace, it soon realizes that it probably lacks the expertise to produce the product. After all, if they knew how to make it, they probably would already be producing it. So how do high-technology companies organize to develop and produce products that far exceed the parameters of current knowledge? They do it by employing what is called "breakthrough technology."

Breakthrough technology has three steps:

1. The company determines what breakthroughs will be needed and makes a list detailing those breakthroughs.

2. The company issues an invitation to all interested and capable parties who might be willing to join together and work on achieving the needed breakthroughs.

3. The company organizes to provide the support needed by the engineers to develop each of the breakthroughs.

These are the same three steps that schools employ when working to collaboratively realize a shared vision. The faculty begins work by meeting together and reviewing the current state of their knowledge, expertise, and thinking on the components that make up the vision. They do this by considering the following question:

FIGURE 13.1

Reflective Writing Prompt for Creating a School Vision

Imagine it is five years from now. Our school has been successful beyond our highest expectations. It is the last week of May, and we are witnessing a student going through a significant "rite of passage," the school's exit exhibition. This is a 20-minute oral presentation (accompanied by artifacts if/when necessary) given before a panel of at least six adults.

The student's assignment is to

• Describe/demonstrate the skills or knowledge that he or she has developed as a consequence of the educational experience at our school.
• Explain/demonstrate how those skills or knowledge were acquired.

In as much detail as possible and using as many concrete examples as you can, relate what you see the student doing and saying.

Source: Sagor, R. D. (1996). *Local control and accountability: How to get it, keep it, and improve school performance* (p. 20). Thousand Oaks, CA: Corwin Press. Copyright © 1996 by Corwin Press. Reprinted by permission of Corwin Press, Inc.

Do we currently know what we need to know to achieve each component of our vision?

Study Groups

One of the more effective ways of producing answers to this question is through the use of study groups (Murphy, 1992). If members of a faculty believe that the professional literature contains important insights into methods or strategies for achieving key portions of their vision, they invite members of their learning community to form a study group to read, discuss, and debate the research and insights of others who have already dealt with similar issues. Occasionally, the work of a study group will unearth an insight or an approach that quickly becomes a consensus choice as the best strategy for meeting the needs of the school's students. When that occurs, the faculty will make a tentative decision to adopt that approach while committing to collect data on their work implementing the strategy and its effectiveness with student learning.

On other occasions, particularly when the issue at hand is perplexing, study groups often conclude that there may be several alternative

FIGURE 13.2

Almeria Middle School Scenario—"The Raphael Story"

Combing his hair, Raphael looks in the mirror. A confident smile crosses his face. Today is an important day. . . .

He begins to mentally prepare for the big event. He remembers to go through all of the steps in the visualization process and focuses on his routine for the day. . . . "Visual imagery really helps me. I am so glad they taught me that technique at Almeria. . . . Almeria! I loved going to school each day. . . . My teachers were so creative. None of that textbook ditto stuff. There was always something new: visual imagery, concept attainment, discovery, discussion, collaborative learning, and debate. . . .

". . . Who would ever have guessed that one of the PALS (People Assisting Learner Success) would change my life forever? I still remember the first day I met my PAL, Draymond. . . . Draymond, like all the other PALS at Almeria, visited the school at least once a week to check up on me. He told me what it was like to work for a living, and he listened to my problems and tried to help. Draymond was always there to meet my emotional needs. . . ."

. . . Coming back to the present, Raphael looks through his school portfolio. He finds writing samples, computer disks, and even videotapes of culminating performances and presentations. He pulls out a narrative report card from 8th grade. . . .

"I was so nervous the first time I was evaluated. What would they have to say about me? My mom was at the meeting along with Draymond, my teachers, my counselor, my advisory teacher, and the resource teacher who helped me in the classroom. . . . Each had a notebook about me describing my academic, emotional, and social growth. I was really behind, but at the same time I knew with everyone's help I could improve. Together we came up with a plan. . . .

". . . Come to think of it, they had a plan for my mom, too. She was invited to become a member of one of the school's problem-solving teams. The team was formed to address the problems of parents who had not yet completed the requirements for a high school diploma. . . .

". . . There were so many connections between classrooms and teachers. . . . I learned so much when they all focused on the same culture and time period. . . . The teachers at Almeria worked so well together and were such good friends. They were always talking together and helping one another make things better for us. They even visited each other in the classroom, to observe lessons and share new ideas. . . .

". . . I remember the poster on the wall of my 6th grade classroom: Inspired Learner, Resourceful Thinker, Effective Communicator, Responsible Citizen, and Productive Worker. Finally, I knew what was expected of me, and my teachers helped by giving the work we did a purpose, a direction. . . .

"I should have known that things were going to be different when I came to Almeria. . . . There were computers, a laser disk player, a video camera, and two different kinds of printers, all in my classroom! There was even virtual

FIGURE 13.2—*continued*

Almeria Middle School Scenario—"The Raphael Story"

reality technology in the library that allowed us to actually interact with events in history and travel to all sections of the world.

"I'll never forget my multimedia project. It tied everything I learned during my three years at Almeria together and challenged me to take my learning one step further. . . . This production would have been impossible if I hadn't learned keyboarding and basic skills in 6th grade, word processing and HyperCard in 7th grade, and how to integrate technology in 8th grade. I learned more than just about computers; I learned how to use interactive multimedia. . . . I knew my project was good even before I presented it because it matched all of the standards for a '6' on the rubric my teacher shared with us. . . ."

. . . With a copy of his college diploma, resume, and several letters of recommendation from former teachers and members of the community, Raphael walks through the door of the IBM Corporation. He announces himself to the receptionist. She is impressed by the young man's confidence and communication skills. As he moves on he is greeted by the personnel director. He extends his hand; she grasps it firmly, and says, "Hi, my name is Latesha. Welcome to IBM."

All of our Raphaels may not have the opportunity to see what happens behind the scenes to make all of this possible. However, action plans have been developed and are being implemented to ensure the future success of Raphael and all Almerians.

—Adapted from material provided by Almeria Middle School in Fontana, California.

---

strategies, each of which appears to have promise. Rather than seeing this as a problematic state of affairs, the existence of competing approaches can be seen as a wonderful opportunity for group learning. A successful high-technology corporation interested in making the breakthroughs necessary to bring an exciting and innovative project to market rarely puts all its eggs in one basket. In the competitive business world, it is far more likely that a company will commission several work groups, each with a different perspective and each attracted to different strategies for making the breakthrough. These work groups then simultaneously pursue the alternative approaches. Good companies realize that it isn't important which strategy or which work team ultimately surfaces the best answer; rather, what matters is that the company acquires the insights needed to bring the visionary product to market.

Pilot Projects

When schools take this perspective, the process in itself helps them develop as efficacious learning communities. It isn't really important whether it turns out that, for example, whole language or phonics or a multifaceted approach is the best way to teach reading. What is important is that, as a community, the school figured out what would best serve their students.

The way that collegial schools manage disagreements over pedagogy or competing perspectives on policy is by framing their disputes as opportunities and then commissioning pilot projects with the understanding that all pilots will be obligated to share what's been learned. Obviously, this process works best in environments in which everyone is open to and desires to learn from one another.

Two Learning Communities

Tomas Rivera Elementary School in Riverside, California, and the West Linn School District in West Linn, Oregon, offer two examples of educational settings in which collegial work has been institutionalized. In the first case, the power of personality was the driving force. In the second case, a powerful idea propelled the district's transformation into a learning community.

By Force of Personality

Tomas Rivera Elementary School is a most exciting place to teach and a very productive place to learn. How did this relatively new school (it opened its doors in the fall of 1995) become such a positive place so quickly? Few knowledgeable sources would hesitate to say that Principal Susan Baltagi was the spark that ignited success at Rivera. It's not that the 40 other professional staff members at Rivera are not each powerful personalities in their own right or that every aspect of the school's program has Susan's imprint on it; but her forceful personality helps keep everyone on track. The pivotal role she plays in this culture of excellence is her unshakable commitment to quality. This commitment was first evidenced in the way she assembled a cadre of teachers who were ready, willing, and able to create a learning organization.

In her previous principalship, Susan became enamored with what she called "action-based research." She encouraged the teachers at her school to conduct inquiries into those areas of practice that they valued,

FIGURE 13.3

Priority Targets at Almeria Middle School

Program Targets
- Rich and diverse instructional strategies
- Expanded roles for parents and community
- Honest, ongoing evaluation of individual student progress in academic, social, and emotional areas
- Decision making and expanded roles for parents and stakeholders
- Professional collaboration
- Integrated curriculum
- Outcome-based accountability system
- Meaning-centered curriculum
- Technology education program

Achievement Targets
- Responsible citizen
- Resourceful thinker
- Effective communicator
- Self-assessment
- Productive worker
- Lifelong technology user
- Perseverance

and she found ways to encourage the sharing of this work both inside the building and around the district. Copies of the thick, spiral-bound compendium of their work still can be found in various corners of this 60,000-student district.

When Rivera was first scheduled to open and Susan was named its planning principal, she determined that action-based research would become a central tenet of work at the school. She negotiated with the human resource department on the precise wording of the job announcement used for recruiting the teachers. It was important to Susan that an interest in conducting disciplined inquiry on teaching be a prerequisite for being selected to teach at Rivera. She was determined to make action-based research a job expectation. If an applicant missed this expectation in the job announcement, the interview left nothing to chance. Not only did Susan ask applicants about their interest in this type of work, but she let them know that everyone at Rivera would be conducting collaborative action research. Consequently, those not interested in doing research on their teaching and their students' learning simply took themselves out of the running.

In April of 1995, the spring before the school opened, the new staff were released from a day of teaching at their current schools to attend an orientation on action-based research. At this point, many educators both in the district office and on the newly assembled staff still didn't quite know what to make of Susan's emphasis on what still seemed like a somewhat esoteric practice. Nevertheless, the new faculty assembled to discuss issues of validity, reliability, and triangulation at a time when most teachers were simply focused on closing down the school year. For her part, Susan was very matter-of-fact about the whole endeavor. She apologized for having a meeting at a bad time of year, but again asserted her belief that everyone would find some aspect of teaching and learning at Rivera that would merit an investment of their intellectual energy. Susan made it clear that she wasn't interested in imposing any particular research agenda on the teachers. As long as their inquiries pertained to matters important to the development of Rivera's children, an individual teacher's research focus had her enthusiastic support. Figure 13.4 lists the projects Rivera teachers conducted during their inaugural year.

I had the privilege of working with the Rivera faculty throughout that first year and experiencing the feelings of efficacy, collegiality, and teamwork that developed as the year progressed and the work continued.

In late August, before the school opened, the teachers selected the initial focus for their research and organized themselves into research teams. The enthusiasm—and stress—related to the tasks ahead, particularly the many issues involved with the opening of a new school, were palpable. Furthermore, there was more than a small amount of concern about what this expectation regarding action-based research was all about. As the stress of opening the school engulfed the faculty, it was only the sheer force of Susan's positive and assertive cheerleading that kept the faculty on track with their research (although privately many teachers were still wondering where this was all leading).

Shortly after winter break, at a time when the research groups had surfaced a great deal of data for analysis, a significant thing happened. Tom Barrett, an evaluation specialist whom Susan had persuaded to become the district office liaison to Rivera (all schools in Riverside have assigned district liaisons), spent a day at the school to work with the teacher researchers. Several groups of teachers approached Tom with queries on how they might organize and make sense of their data. Tom rolled up his sleeves and provided an impromptu workshop on using database and spreadsheet software to display, organize, and analyze classroom data. He pledged to continue to be available for technical assistance as needed.

FIGURE 13.4

Tomas Rivera Elementary School
Action-Based Research Projects, 1995–96

- The effectiveness of various spelling strategies
- The transfer of skills acquired in the communication lab
- The development of independent learners
- The development of lifelong fitness skills
- The development of social skills and impact on academic achievement
- The effectiveness of various approaches to reading on performance and attitude
- Impact of visual arts study on problem solving across the curriculum

---

The importance of this timely assistance from a "critical friend" can't be overstated. The message it conveyed to these busy teacher researchers was that they weren't alone in their work. In fact, Tom, Susan, and Debbie Mestas, Susan's assistant, modeled "servant leadership" (Sergiovanni, 1992) at its best throughout the project. The behavior of these leaders made it clear that helping Rivera's teachers succeed with the research process was their top priority. Furthermore, Rivera's "outside" critical friends demonstrated that being on-call consultants to teachers was, perhaps, the most fulfilling aspect of their jobs.

In Project LEARN's research with schools that were implementing collaborative action research, we have seen this pattern repeated over and over again. When the push for action research is initiated by administrators, the success and longevity of the effort is directly related to the support (tangible and emotional) that teachers receive from their leaders. When teachers feel that their research efforts are recognized and appreciated by building administrators, they are more than willing to go the extra mile. Conversely, it is a safe bet that teachers will avoid committing to tasks (such as action research) that appear tangential when and if that work seems neither valued nor appreciated by their supervisors. That first winter at Rivera demonstrated clearly that when the going got rough, the support became abundant!

The crowning moment of Rivera's opening year came on April 29, 1996, when the school hosted the first Tomas Rivera Educational Research Conference. The conference took place on a staff development day. The program consisted of each research team presenting their work to their colleagues and several dozen guests from the district, neighboring districts, and local universities. If anyone remained skeptical regarding the purpose, importance, or interest in action-based research, that skepticism was put to rest by 3:00 p.m. that afternoon. As the faculty took off to celebrate their success at a local tavern, they weren't just celebrating the relief that comes from accomplishing something new and overcoming their fears; they were toasting the birth of a learning community.

As spring and summer progressed, more frosting was added to their cake. One of the teachers was selected as the district's "beginning teacher of the year," the school was asked to share its staff development model with other schools in the district, and its unique approach to class-size reduction was adopted as a district model. Although the staff accepted each of those external validations with great appreciation, nothing satisfied them as much as being part of the team they had created. Furthermore, the success of their students on the mandated statewide achievement test, which resulted from their teamwork, stood as powerful testimony to their collective efficacy.

By Force of an Idea

When Dea Cox accepted the superintendency at the West Linn (Oregon) School District (later renamed the West Linn-Wilsonville School District) in 1978, there wasn't much in the academic program that set this historic district apart from its neighbors. Stability, tradition, a senior staff, and aging buildings were the West Linn School District's major claims to fame. Dea came to the district with a well-deserved reputation as an innovator. In the past he had led a number of nationally recognized innovative curriculum projects and had transformed one poor rural district into a virtual magnet for federal discretionary funds; he was now returning to the Pacific Northwest from a stint as an intern at Harvard University. It would have been logical for folks at West Linn to expect Dea to ride into town with a host of high-profile programs to revitalize this sleepy and contented district.

Although that might have been a logical prediction, considering Dea's past, it turned out to be off target. Dea returned from Harvard with a radical idea. His current thinking contrasted both with his past leadership approach and with the tenor of the times. He now believed that it wasn't programs that produced educational excellence; it was personnel that made the difference between a good and a great district. Following that simple premise, the organizing idea for Dea's tenure at West Linn was called the "people strategy." Specifically, the people strategy was a commitment to create an outstanding school district by attracting, nurturing, and supporting good people as they strove to do their best work.

Twenty years later, the West Linn-Wilsonville School District is a living testament to that powerful idea. During a period when adoption of programs was the name of the game, when district public relations releases from most neighboring districts featured a listing of the "nationally recognized" programs being adopted and implemented, West Linn was publicly celebrating professionalism. The district's staff development program was vast and well financed. It encompassed the ideas of all the educational circuit riders of the time. Sessions sponsored by the district included references to Hunter, Gardner, and Glasser, but attendees were always cautioned that these ideas were not gospel, and teacher evaluation would not be based on a faithful demonstration of the beliefs of Madeline Hunter, Lee Canter, Rudolf Dreikurs, or anyone else. Rather, in West Linn, teacher evaluation was to be based on evidence of teacher learning.

Teachers were granted an entitlement, paid by the district, to purchase as many as 24 graduate credits annually. Dea publicly expressed his hope that many teachers would use this grant to obtain master's degrees or even doctorates. When a community member would challenge him on the expense (paying for the classes and also giving teachers a bump on the salary schedule), he responded that the more West Linn's teachers knew and the better educated they were, the greater the benefit to the district's students.

Tenure began to be called by its nickname—"the million dollar decision." It was so named for the amount of money the board of education was encumbering for the future salary and benefits of a permanent teacher. For this reason, the district wrote a policy stating that the granting of tenure was reserved only for those who had used their first three years in the district to demonstrate (through what is now called a teaching portfolio) "excellence as a teacher and as a collaborative professional." Each spring the community, the teachers union, and the school board feted the newly tenured teachers at a catered reception. The event was held to express the appreciation of the community for the fact that these great educators would be spending the rest of their careers assisting with the "raising of the community's children."

Over the next 20 years, consistent adherence to the intent of the people strategy by Dea, his successor, Superintendent Roger Woehl, several dozen board members, and an evolving administrative team has enabled these values to become deeply ingrained in the district. It is now hard to find anyone who can even remember the district before the people strategy was in place. District schools are regularly visited by educators from throughout the country who are attracted by the innovative work of the teachers. What they hear surprises them. They notice that many of the best programs—the very ones with the regional and national reputations—are not implemented across the district, but only in those schools where the faculty and community have deemed them appropriate.

What is most remarkable is that this doesn't reflect a laissez-faire attitude by the district, and it doesn't place the schools in competition with each other. Unlike a magnet school strategy, where competition for students drives reform, each school and each classroom in West Linn-Wilsonville is a laboratory where ideas are tested, grown, and adopted if and when they fit the context, and then the results are shared. The district's 400 teachers are spread across 11 schools and are all members of an extended learning community. Assistant Superintendent Jane Stickney likens school improvement in West Linn-Wilsonville to an "ongoing conversation" with all members of the community invited to join in, if and when they feel it appropriate.

Each spring, the district hosts its annual Celebration of Inquiry. More than 600 people attend the event, including all the district's certificated staff. Attendees participate in an educational conference with more than 75 separate breakout sessions, as well as keynote speeches, catered meals, and exhibitors. They may earn academic credit supplied from a local university. Participants may well think they were attending a high-powered conference sponsored by a professional association. In fact, they are! The major difference, however, between this and other "national" conferences is that all the sessions are presented by members of the West Linn-Wilsonville School District professional staff, and the research findings being shared are the result of research done in local schools and local classrooms.

Teachers learning from the research of teachers: this is what has become the norm at Tomas Rivera and at West Linn-Wilsonville. The end result of what was created in one venue by the force of personality—Susan Baltagi's commitment—and at the other through the force of an idea—the people strategy—is the same, a deeply rooted learning community. Each year when I attend the end-of-year programs in California and Oregon, what strikes me is the total absence of one-upmanship and defensiveness. In these cauldrons of competing educational ideas, competition among the professionals is nonexistent. In fact, in these communities of learners, competition among ideas has become a never-ending source of renewable energy.

With all of the autonomy in programs and processes, what binds the educators in these two very different places is a collective passion to find out what is best for their students. Furthermore, with each step they take in that direction, the teachers in these schools are reinforced in their belief that they can and will prevail. Sometimes I even think I hear the teachers chanting, "I think I can, I think I can, I think I can . . . ."

14 Inducting Teachers into a Culture of Inquiry

The research on professional socialization and induction of new teachers has made it clear that beginning teachers' first experiences are the most powerful ones of their careers (Veenman 1984). Furthermore, the perspectives and values encountered during that induction year tend to become internalized and maintained throughout an educator's career. That fact by itself may go a long way toward explaining the low levels of professional efficacy observed with many of today's teachers. If teachers start out teaching in an environment where the organizational structures, the attitudes of colleagues, and the demands on time emphasize only the limitations on what can be accomplished, it is logical that they will end up facing work with a sense of futility.

Peer Coaching

To respond to this sad situation and to meet the induction and professional development needs of new teachers, many thoughtful educators and policymakers have lobbied for funding for mentoring programs to assist beginning teachers with their introduction into the teaching profession. One element of most new teacher programs is mentoring by an experienced colleague using a *peer coaching* model. The rationale is that a rookie teacher can gain a great deal by observing others and by being observed and getting feedback from a more experienced colleague.

This certainly seems like a good idea, and over the past 15 years, educators have gained quite a bit of experience using this model. How-ever, the evidence suggests that in spite of near universal acceptance of its worthiness, most peer coaching initiatives fade once the mandate, the funding, or the requirement disappears. All of this raises a question:

If teachers feel that peer coaching is such a productive and positive use of their time, why don't they continue to engage in peer coaching when it is no longer required?

Certainly, one reason for the short life span of coaching initiatives is the amount of time that productive peer coaching requires. This is a concern that shouldn't be minimized. However, as with other aspects of teaching, if an activity is meaningful and attractive enough, teachers find time to sustain the effort.

A better explanation for the difficulty individual teachers and school systems have in institutionalizing this type of collegial work may be the manner in which new teachers experience the peer coaching relationship. Their experience with coaching often runs counter to the prevailing norms of public school teaching. It has often been said that teaching is one of the world's most private acts. That assertion holds more than a little truth. As teachers grow accustomed to conducting their work in solitude inside a system that tacitly adheres to the belief that things are just fine as they are and that the best way to get along is to "see no evil, hear no evil, and speak no evil," then opening teaching to the scrutiny of others is quite risky.

These problems are amplified in new teacher programs. It's not that anyone would disagree that rookies can use the assistance of a coach (a more seasoned colleague). It's that maintaining a mentor-mentee relationship is difficult in the long run. For good reasons, new teachers look forward to a day when they will no longer be seen as neophytes in need of the helping hands of "wiser" superiors. Furthermore, the norm of equity that pervades most schools is such that the veterans also look forward to the day when their "beginner" colleagues will pull their own weight and become just "one of us." Is it any wonder then, that a relationship built upon the assumption that one partner is superior to another is hard to sustain?

Several years ago when consulting with California educators working on a beginning teacher support program, we began searching for a positive way to introduce collaborative action research into schools where the culture supported the norm of individualism. Like peer coaching, collaborative action research is an idea filled with appeal for teachers. However, unlike peer coaching, which can appear easy on the surface but later turns out to be quite difficult, the research process often appears daunting when first introduced and is seen as manageable only after one gains confidence and experience. Knowing that the scope of action research often appears intimidating, we began a search for a mechanism that would encourage teachers to test the waters and get their feet wet before taking the plunge into full-blown collaborative action research.

We wanted to find a strategy that would enable teachers to get a taste of the efficacy-building benefit of using data with their instructional decision making, but that wouldn't require engaging in all the activities of a collaborative action research project. Our search resulted in the creation of a developmental strategy that would encourage the growth of action researchers while simultaneously deepening an educator's willingness to continue in collegial peer coaching relationships.

Informal Collaborative Action Research

The collaborative action research model is based upon collaboratively launched inquiries into significant issues of practice. The result of these pursuits has been shown to improve teacher and student performance as well as enhance professional efficacy. Even with all of that going for it, we realized that two groups of teachers needed a safe "first-timers" strategy: (1) beginning teachers and (2) veteran teachers with low efficacy. We recognized that there were good reasons why both rookies and low-efficacy teachers would be reluctant to volunteer to become teacher researchers, and we felt that what was needed was an approach that would accommodate projects of less complexity but with high potential for success, thus enhancing efficacy.

We reasoned that if our strategy was to serve as an introduction to collaborative action research, it needed to be true to the structure of the action research process and it needed to involve collegial work. However, it also had to minimize the most threatening aspects of collegial work and had to be attractive to those who hadn't had good experiences working side by side with other professionals.

Later, this work was incorporated into a distance learning master's program at Marygrove College in Michigan. At Marygrove, we called the first step of this developmental process "informal" collaborative action research (Lerner, 1997). Anyone well versed in peer coaching models will likely note that informal collaborative action research (as we defined it) is a very close cousin of peer coaching. Figure 14.1 compares and contrasts peer coaching with both informal collaborative action research and collaborative action research as discussed in the first two parts of this book.

When these three models are compared, their many common features jump out. All three programs focus on the improvement of

FIGURE 14.1

Comparison of Three Capacity-Building Models

Informal Collaborative Action Research	Peer Coaching	Formal Collaborative Action Research
1. Problem formulation: The researcher chooses an aspect of his/her teaching to gather information about.	**1. Problem identification:** The coach and coachee agree on an aspect of the coachee's teaching to work on.	**1. Problem formulation:** The team of researchers reflect on and choose a topic for research that they collectively find meaningful.
2. Plan for data collection: The researcher decides on the observational data the coresearcher should obtain during a classroom observation.	**2. Preconference:** A joint decision is made on what information the coach will observe and report to the coachee.	**2. Plan for data collection:** The team agrees on a triangulated plan to collect data on questions of mutual interest.
3. Collection of data: The coresearcher observes in classroom and collects data agreed to in step 2.	**3. Observation:** The coach observes in classroom and collects data agreed to in step 2.	**3. Collection of data:** The team works at assembling a variety of pieces of data to answer the research questions.
4. Analysis of data: The researcher draws inferences and conclusions from the data presented and collected by the coresearcher.	**4. Postconference:** The coach and coachee discuss the data and draw inferences and conclusions.	**4. Analysis of data:** The team looks for patterns of findings and draws conclusions from the assembled data.
5. Reporting of results: The researcher shares orally or in writing what was learned with one or more colleagues.	**5. Reporting of results:** The postconference (step 4) is the reporting process.	**5. Reporting of results:** The team prepares a report of the findings and understandings derived from the study and shares it with colleagues.
6. Action planning: The researcher makes decisions, informed by the data on changes in practice.	**6. Action planning:** The coach and coachee jointly make decisions on changes in practice.	**6. Action planning:** The team confers on the changes in the practice that might occur as a consequence of their analysis of the data.

instruction, use teacher-collected data, and involve the collaborative work of peers. There are, however, four crucial distinctions between these three models that merit further discussion. These distinctions can be considered in terms of four issues:

- Who directs the process?
- What types of data are collected?
- Who is responsible for analyzing and interpreting the data?
- Where are results reported?

Who's directs the process? In informal collaborative action research, the teacher researcher is the quarterback, the person empowered to call all of the plays. In traditional research settings this person would be called the "principal investigator" (PI). The PI selects the topics for study and uses the assistance of his or her coresearcher in the same manner that a professor might use a "research assistant" (RA), a subordinate working under the PI's direction. In traditional peer coaching, the coach (the mentor) calls the play or the plays (for example, the focus of the observations), or the focus is mutually selected. Similarly, in formal collaborative action research, the focus of an investigation is jointly established.

What types of data are collected? In informal collaborative action research and in peer coaching, the data collected is observational in nature. These inquiries usually focus on phenomena of practice that can be readily observed, often in the course of a short classroom visit. In formal collaborative action research, many different forms of data are sought and used for triangulation purposes.

Who is responsible for analyzing and interpreting the data? As was the case with the selection of a focus, in informal collaborative action research the teacher researcher is the person in charge of analysis. This is as it should be. After all, if it is the PI's questions that the data is supposed to answer, then the PI should be in charge of the analysis. The research assistant may be present during analysis, but this person works in a clearly subordinate role to the PI. In peer coaching and formal collaborative action research, the uncovering of the story in the data as well as the discussions on the meaning behind the data should occur in a fully equal and collaborative mode.

Where are results reported? In both peer coaching and informal collaborative action research, the inquiry has only one audience: the individual whose classroom was observed. However, in formal collaborative action research, it is hoped that others in the larger school and educational community will be influenced by the findings.

These distinctions make clear the developmental aspect of this strategy. It begins with the safety of informal action research, with the observed teacher in control. Only later does the teacher move up to peer coaching and finally to full-blown collaborative action research. By employing a developmental approach for easing into peer coaching and collaborative action research, these sometimes intimidating processes can become longstanding features of a school. Perhaps more important, in deliberately working their way up a developmental ladder, new professionals can experience some of the efficacy building of collaborative action research during their crucial induction year.

The four distinctions can be reduced to two essential issues: *Who's in charge?* and *Who conducts the analysis?* Both of these issues merit greater discussion.

Who's in Charge?

Although new teachers are often disinclined to complain about their novice status in the coaching relationship, they cannot escape the fact that they are being cast (often publicly) in a subordinate role. This is particularly true if they are involved in a mentor-teaching relationship. This situation isn't accidental. The rationale behind these programs is to provide a more experienced set of eyes to look for things the novice might be overlooking. Although this undoubtedly can prove helpful in the short run, it isn't long before the novice wants to say, "Thank you very much for your help, but I am now capable of standing on my own two feet!" Noticing this, Andy Hargreaves of University of Toronto commented during a presentation, "Maybe they should be called 'tormentors,' not 'mentors.'"

Now, contrast this with the informal collaborative action research model. Here new teachers are placed in charge of their own growth. The novices are the ones deciding on the focus area (need) and on the specific issues that might benefit from more information. Perhaps more important, the informal model empowers the new teacher through the provision of a "research assistant." Rather than having the mentor program be a constant reminder of skills the teacher lacks, the presence of the veteran's (the research assistant's) eyes and ears becomes an expression of the investment the school has made in the teacher's personal, self-directed growth.

Who Conducts the Analysis?

The question of who conducts the analysis is another area of potential difficulty that arises when jumping too soon into peer coaching with new teachers. In the best peer coaching models (Robbins, 1991; Joyce and Showers, 1982), two equal professionals discuss the phenomenon being observed (the teaching episode) as colleagues. Although this is a noble goal, it is difficult to achieve, especially when there is a significant disparity in experience. It is only to be expected that the novice will defer to the "superior" knowledge of the veteran. Only if a coach/mentor has the interpersonal skills of a Rogerian therapist will the post-observation discussions provide an equal and empowered voice for the novice.

The delineation of roles (PI and RA) in the informal collaborative action research model is especially valuable here. The data that the "research assistant" brings to the conference is data that was "commissioned" by the PI (the novice teacher). That fact alone underscores who owns the data and therefore makes it clear who should direct the interpretation phase.

There is no reason, when using the informal collaborative action research model in a mentor program, why the roles of veteran and novice couldn't or shouldn't be reversed. Experienced teachers often find that they need an additional set of eyes and ears to look at an important aspect of their teaching. When and if the veteran requests such help, then true reciprocity in this collegial peer relationship can be achieved, regardless of any initial differences in the status of the players.

When I served as a high school principal, I offered my services as a "research assistant" to first-year teachers. At their request, I would go to their rooms and collect any data they wanted me to help them retrieve. That offer of servant leadership, usually made within the first few weeks of a teacher's experience on our staff, paid dividends for years to come. When I reflected on this, I suspected it was my willingness to work *for* them that made the difference. It underscored the view that in our school anyone with a valid question was encouraged to become a principal investigator, and anyone with a willingness to help could be a researcher assistant. This helped set the stage for long-term comfort with peer coaching and collaborative action research.

When a school decides to start out with informal collaborative action research, with the roles of principal investigator and research assistant assumed independent of employment status, work with peers is seen as less risky and doesn't become just an aversive reminder of one's inferred inadequacies.

Although this discussion has focused on using informal collaborative action research as a means to acclimate beginning teachers to a culture of inquiry, it is equally suited as a first step for building a long-term commitment to peer coaching and other forms of collegial sharing by an experienced but individualistic faculty. After one or two cycles though the informal collaborative action research process, novice researchers begin to feel empowered, in charge of their development, and respected as colleagues by other professionals. As a result they become willing to take the risks inherent in formal collaborative action research (as well as in a long-term peer coaching relationship).

Other Approaches to Induction

In addition to peer coaching and the informal collaborative action research model described above, other approaches can provide effective means to introduce educators to the benefits of action research. These include classes for new teachers that provide training and support for teacher research, school-university partnerships implemented through professional development schools, and university requirements that incorporate action research projects.

New Teacher Classes

When I was a principal, our school sponsored a "new teacher seminar" each fall. The district gave graduate credit for the seminar, which was available to any teacher, novice or veteran, new to our building (Sagor & Barnett, 1994). The syllabus for this class consisted of those instructional issues that the participants deemed meaningful. The seminar leader, the principal

- Provided training on data-gathering techniques to be used in classroom observations.
- Arranged for substitutes so that participants could observe each other.
- Conducted literature reviews, if desired by participants.
- Stayed out of their way.

By winter break, each new teacher in our school had received assistance from at least a half dozen colleagues acting as their research assistants on their informal action research dealing with issues chosen because they were a personal professional priority. In addition, the new teachers were the recipients of logistical support on their priorities from their principal. This type of program teaches as much by process as content. What we wanted to convey was both deliberate and simple: we wanted the new staff to see that they were in a school where everyone (including the principal) was committed to investing in the self-directed development of each member of the staff.

Professional Development Schools

Professional development schools (PDSs) are partnerships between school districts and universities created to enhance the development of teaching and learning and help with the preparation of teachers. The basic theory, as developed by the Holmes Group (1990) and Levine (1988), is built upon an analogy to university medical centers. Medical centers are places where the medical profession simultaneously trains new physicians, conducts important research, and provides cutting-edge treatment for patients.

Traditionally the assignment of student teachers or interns in education has been haphazard at best, with the major considerations being the cooperative teacher's willingness to host a student teacher and the proximity of the school to the university campus. An innovative model explored by the Collaborative Professional Development School Project at Washington State University's Vancouver, Washington, campus created an additional goal for the internship year. Under this model, the cooperating teacher assisted the intern in developing the habits of teacher research. Just as potential residents in medicine might look for assignment to a residency where they could work with a top researcher working on breakthrough techniques, the professional development school sought to provide that same type of induction opportunity for beginning teachers.

The process consisted of having veteran teacher researchers who were working in the professional development school sites make requests for interns who shared an interest in their research agenda: for example, student assessment, inclusion, problem-solving techniques in math, and so on. When an appropriate placement was made, both partners received several significant benefits. The interns were able to explore an important educational issue along with their experienced mentors. Also, the interns could use their collaborative research as the basis for their master's theses. The cooperating teachers also received valuable benefits. They received help with the ever-present issue of time. The interns willingly helped with data collection (after all, the interns would be writing theses and getting credit for their work), and the interns provided the cooperating teachers some relief from other instructional responsibilities. Finally, by writing up the research and conducting the necessary literature reviews, the interns provided a service that is hard to fit into a busy teacher's schedule. This is precisely the type of support most teachers say they need if they are to regularly engage in action research. Perhaps the most important thing about this approach, however, was that the interns' first experience in a public school classroom was provided by an inquiring and data-driven educator.

University Requirements

Increasingly, universities are designing their graduate programs to include action research requirements. This is a wonderful opportunity to help experienced teachers enjoy the benefits of teacher research in a supportive environment.

At Marygrove College in Michigan several hundred students each year are enrolled in a distance-learning master's program. These students are expected to complete two collaborative action research projects as part of their degree program. Marygrove follows the developmental model presented at the beginning of this chapter. The student's first project follows the informal collaborative action research model, and the second project requires the student to complete each of the elements of a full-blown collaborative action research project (including multiple data sources and a literature review).

Easing the Way

A basic premise behind this book has been that two minds are almost always better than one, and three are even better than two. Clearly, professional growth, efficacy, and enhanced learning grow best in school cultures that encourage comfortable and fearless interchanges among colleagues. However, just as we've come to recognize the need for developmentalism when introducing our students to threatening new tasks, as school leaders we need to consider the use of sequential, low-risk, and developmentally appropriate practices for our staff development efforts.

Using strategies such as informal collaborative action research or the introduction of collaborative action research as part of student teaching makes crossing the individualistic cultural chasm that much easier for classroom teachers. More important, such practices can set the stage for the building of a truly collegial school culture.

15 The Demands of Accountability: Integrating Action Research into District Practice

Teachers are usually not looking for more work. For this reason, until they have had a positive experience with action research, many have little reason to volunteer to take on this or any other additional tasks. So what might a school or a district do to encourage veteran members of their professional staff to take the plunge and become teacher researchers?

Tying Inquiry to Staff Development

One novel and promising approach is the one used in the Killeen (Texas) Independent School District. KISD is a 30,000-student district serving the Fort Hood army base and the diverse residents of this sprawling central Texas city. The Killeen Board of Education and Charles Patterson, the superintendent of schools, have long believed that staff development is the key to school improvement. As a consequence, the district annually invests in providing a rich menu of training opportunities. The programs offered each summer and throughout the school year feature some of the most sought-after teacher educators in North America.

The school leaders in Killeen are very much aware of the sorry history of implementation following traditional, one-shot, "egg on the wall" inservice sessions.[1] Consequently they sought a strategy that would

---

[1]Madeline Hunter used to talk about traditional inservice sessions as throwing egg on the wall and hoping that something would stick!

encourage teachers to make long-term commitments to learn, work with, and ultimately adopt and adapt cutting-edge practices into their teaching repertoires. In 1996 this desire gave rise to what is now called "Goal III" (its name derived from its placement on a list of annual district goals). Teachers who express an interest in any of the district's priorities for staff development are invited to apply for a Goal III grant.

Becoming a Goal III teacher is much more then being a mere grant recipient. Participation in Goal III is a contractual agreement between the teacher and the district. In exchange for participating in a top-quality inservice program during the summer, making a commitment to actively participate as a member of a "strategy network," and agreeing to complete an action research project, the staff member receives a stipend from the district.

Each year the menu of possibilities is quite extensive. For example, in 1998–99 strategy networks were in place for technology, cooperative learning, multiple intelligences, 4MAT learning styles, New Jersey writing project, math workshop, P.E., using the calculator, and other areas of interest. After attending a week-long inservice offering of their choice, all Goal III participants receive training in how to conduct collaborative action research. Later all participants are expected to conduct an inquiry of their choosing on an issue arising from the inservice program attended. Monthly networking sessions become opportunities to discuss emerging issues with other educators working on the implementation of the same instructional strategies. These meetings also serve as support groups for the implementers, as well as venues for routine sharing of data and emerging findings from their action research.

A district leader is assigned to facilitate each network, and these network coordinators stay "on call" as critical friends to the Goal III teachers. The network coordinators assist participants with advice on research methods, feedback from classroom observations, and in the preparation of their final action research reports. In addition to sharing their action research reports with members of their network, the teachers present their reports at their school, through the school's site-based management council.

The time, energy, and effort expended by Goal III teachers far exceeds the compensation (a stipend) they receive, yet teacher enthusiasm for this work has stayed strong and is growing. Over time, each network takes on the flavor of a unique learning community. What is unique about these communities is that their members are not joined by grade level or attendance zone, but by a common professional interest in an instructional approach. The value of membership in these communities is apparent by the fact that most Goal III teachers re-enlist for participation in additional cycles. Now several former Goal III teachers are serving as network coordinators. Through the Goal III strategy, Killeen ISD is consciously and simultaneously building a set of overlapping learning communities in the networks, in the buildings, and in the district, each powered by an ever-growing supply of local expertise.

If the impact of this strategy is projected over the long haul (10 years or more), the internal capacity of KISD will be enormously enhanced. This should become a district with significant expertise in both research methodology and cutting-edge curriculum and instructional practices. Perhaps more important, involvement with inquiry will have become a routine facet of practice, carried out at several levels of the organization.

Professional Growth Evaluation

Teachers, administrators, and school boards are increasingly frustrated over the limited value of traditional teacher evaluation. The procedural requirements for acceptable summative evaluation are not only time consuming for supervisors but are often perceived by teachers as simply another hoop to jump through. Worst of all, traditional evaluation techniques have been shown to provide no demonstrable benefit for students. These shortcomings are largely due to the fact that traditional evaluation programs were designed to facilitate employment decisions (retention, promotion, removal, tenure, probation), not for improving the professional work of teachers who are already competent. Although no one would argue that valid summative evaluations are not needed for employment decisions, the vast majority of public school teachers are already tenured (or have some other form of permanent status), are performing at or above expectations, and have little need to go through the annual evaluation "show and tell" ritual.

For these reasons, many states and districts have been offering opportunities for teachers to engage in and document their professional growth in lieu of a traditional summative evaluation. Action research fits very comfortably into these types of professional growth evaluation systems.

Unlike *summative evaluation,* which is done to assist with employment decisions, the rationale behind *formative evaluation* is solely to assist in the development of the employee. Because action research (as defined in this book) is also a process for building a teacher's knowledge and skill while enhancing empowerment and efficacy, it is fully compatible with the goals of formative evaluation.

When using action research for professional growth evaluation, the teacher follows the sequential steps of the collaborative action research process (problem formulation, planning for data collection, collection of data, analysis of data, action planning, and reporting). Most professional growth evaluation processes ask the teacher's supervisor to play a supportive role. Research has shown that the quality of that involvement is a major factor in the success of these programs. One manageable and productive role for supervisors in professional growth evaluation is to serve as the teacher's research assistant (as described in Chapter 14).

Professional growth evaluation programs have now been in operation for a number of years, and several instructive lessons have emerged regarding their effectiveness. The two findings that I find most relevant for our purpose (the development of inquiring, efficacious educators and learning communities) have to do with the role of the supervisor and the organizational context in professional growth evaluation.

The Role of the Supervisor

Allen Hughes (1992) studied the use of professional growth evaluation in a school district that had been recognized by its state department of education for exemplary use of professional growth evaluation. Hughes began his research convinced he would find evidence that instructional practices had improved throughout the district and that student learning had been enhanced as a consequence of faculty involvement in this teacher-directed professional growth process.

To his surprise, he found little evidence of change in teacher behavior and no change in student performance after several years of involvement with the program. Was this a result of a fatal flaw in the model? Did this mean that empowering teachers with decision making over their own professional development was a poor idea? And, if it was a good idea, why wasn't there more evidence of benefit?

After interviewing both administrators and teachers, Hughes noticed some interesting patterns:

• Supervisors viewed having their teachers participate in professional growth evaluation as giving them a year off from their traditional evaluation duties.

• Most supervisors were unable to recall the goals or the focus of the work engaged in by the teachers they had supervised, even though they were required to approve and sign off on the completion of projects.

• Most supervisors reported spending very little time with the teachers on their professional growth projects, and the time that they recalled spending was almost exclusively devoted to procedural compliance.

• Most teachers reported favorable attitudes toward the process, but this was primarily because it provided them relief from the chore of traditional evaluation.

• Most of the projects undertaken by the teachers were (by the teacher's own admission) matters of little significance to either teaching or learning.

• No changes in student performance, either positive or negative, could be traced to the professional growth option program.

Hughes theorized that the supervisors' failure to demonstrate meaningful interest in the teachers' work implied to the teachers that their work wasn't particularly valued. Consequently, the teachers made a rational decision to take the most expedient and painless route through the process. Although the professional growth model of evaluation held great potential, the findings from this study supported the old proverb, "Little ventured, little gained."

Organizational Context

Disturbed by these findings, Judy Reault (1998) conducted a follow-up study in two other districts in the same state that were also reputed to have quality professional growth evaluation programs. The districts she studied differed in some significant ways and consequently had very different experiences with this evaluation model.

One district, with the reputation for the better program, had things organized beautifully. A required orientation to professional growth evaluation was conducted each fall by an officer of the teachers union. The teachers received a handbook with all the information they could possibly need to guide them through the process. The supervisors had their own time line outlining requirements along the way. Finally, the district put a reporting system in place that served to hold everyone accountable and to keep everyone on track. This district expected that the chosen focuses for teacher inquiries would be the furtherance of some school or district goal. Because the teacher inquiry process was an important district priority, a budget was put into place to help teachers with special expenses.

The other district implemented the program in a far more laissez-faire and less costly manner. It did not clearly delineate the roles and responsibilities of the supervisor or the expectations of the teachers. All that Reault could find to describe the program was a simple paragraph in the collective bargaining agreement.

Surprisingly, Reault found little impact anywhere in the first district. In fact, voluntary entrance into the professional growth process declined each year. Even with all the district commitment, many teachers reported to Reault that the process was "just another set of hoops" for teachers to jump through. Surprisingly, in the second district, the success of the program was far greater, but (as one might expect with such a loose program), its effectiveness differed significantly from building to building. The program was most successful in those buildings where there was no principal turnover and where the principal expressed support for the program. Each year more and more teachers voluntarily signed up, the focus of their projects became more challenging and even more time consuming, the degree of cross-teacher collaboration increased, and most surprising, the teachers (although not requested to do so) began selecting projects that related directly to the school's goals.

Using Bacharach and Mundell's (1993) "Logic of Action" framework, Reault concluded that these two districts differed significantly in "organizational context." District number one was an organization marked by "bureaucratic accountability," while district number two had a culture of "professional autonomy." Although these districts differed significantly, the type of teachers in both districts who were most likely to volunteer for the professional growth program were teachers who sought personal satisfaction through "work success." Reault concluded that when teachers are seeking satisfaction through "work success" but happen to work in environments marked by "bureaucratic accountability," they tend to see professional growth evaluation as simply another bureaucratic mechanism and reject it. She saw this repeatedly in district number one, where teachers reported that "it took too much time," and "it simply wasn't worth it." Conversely, in an environment of "professional autonomy" (such as in district number two), these same types of teachers willingly invested their time and energy in their chosen projects. Moreover, and ironically, the projects the teachers invested in district number two were, more often then not, supportive of the school's collective vision.

Program Quality Reviews and Accreditation

Just as traditional teacher evaluation has been found wanting, not living up to its stated objectives, similar shortcomings have been found in the processes used for school accreditation and program quality reviews (PQRs). Currently, most secondary schools and an increasing number of elementary schools are being required to go through periodic accreditation. In addition, many states now require regular program quality reviews for all schools. In the past, accreditation meant measuring a school's compliance with a checklist of standards. The standards usually focused on inputs, not outcomes. The logic of this approach was that if all the proper inputs were in place, then the school must be on the right track.

In time, many schools and districts became frustrated, recognizing that school improvement was more than counting the number of books in the library, the nature of the course offerings, and the distribution of faculty. This gave rise in many locales to alternative forms of accreditation as well as new approaches to state-mandated program reviews. These new models are based on the presentation of data on school improvement efforts and the accomplishment of learning goals. Whereas the old paradigm was concerned with inputs, the new paradigm focuses on outcomes. That change opens the door for using collaborative action research in a school's program review and accreditation work.

From my years as a high school teacher, I recall quite well the two years of the accreditation process (the self-study year followed by the visitation year). Functionally, those years were a time-out from all of our discretionary school improvement work. Collecting data for an accreditation report took everyone's full time and energy and focused the faculty not on our priorities, but on the accreditation criteria. In many ways it felt like we were getting ready for a test. We had a study guide, a 200-page manual from the accreditation association, and our task was simply to write down the "correct" answer for each of the questions. The following year a group of outside reviewers would arrive with the "answer key" and score us. It seemed to me and my colleagues that we were spending a lot of our valuable time making our school conform to a model of excellence that seemed very mechanical. Accreditation showed no respect for the local context. It was as though every critical component of quality schooling had been generalized, and we simply had to fit our school into a preset mold. It hardly seemed like a productive use of human resources. It is not surprising that busy teachers develop negative feelings toward accreditation and program quality reviews if they are perceived as stealing valuable time from other, more important, pursuits.

I've argued that the best way for action researchers to avoid the problem of diverting finite time and energy to low-priority efforts is by being "selfish" about their research focus (Sagor, 1993). I believe teachers should look at action research as a "self-indulgent pursuit." I urge teachers to do everything in their power to keep others from assigning them a particular research topic. Rather, I urge teachers to focus on an issue or issues that are of passionate personal concern. I find this strategy works because teachers have always been willing to invest in projects that meet these criteria. That is logical, because time invested in matters of personal interest always pays off. When we work on our own passions, we become more effective aligning our priorities, and that, in turn, allows us to build our sense of professional efficacy. I believe this helps explain why Judy Reault found so much more enthusiasm among the teachers who worked in an environment supportive of professional autonomy.

This may all sound nice, but what if working on a collective school-wide need is a requirement? What if teachers simply "have to" produce an accountability report? How do we justify asking teachers to invest in a collaborative project when there is so little time and energy to spare?

Killing Multiple Birds with the Same Stone

As a child I remember my mother telling me that the task before me really wasn't that bad; I just needed to learn how to "kill two birds with one stone." If the only accountability demands on a faculty's time were those they placed upon themselves, the investment required for collaborative action research would never seem too great. But that is rarely the case. As mentioned earlier, practically every secondary school in North America is required to go through an elaborate accreditation process, and in many localities elementary accreditation is fast becoming the norm. In addition, most states and provinces are requiring either a standardization process from schools or participation in a "quality review process." Furthermore, in return for the autonomy granted through site-based management, many large districts are demanding school improvement plans (SIPs) backed by elaborate annual evaluations on progress. Faced with all these external accountability requirements, it is not surprising that the teachers in many schools cry out, "Enough is enough!"

They are right. After all, there are only 24 hours in a day. However, with a little creativity, school leaders can find ways to not only kill two birds with one stone, but create increased empowerment and efficacy for their teachers by doing so. Accomplishing this will require attention to a sequence of four steps:

1. Validate the school vision

2. Profile the current status
3. Commission or conduct action research on goal areas
4. Generate a composite annual report

Validating the School Vision

Chapter 13 detailed a process for generating a school vision using the scenario writing process. In that chapter I argued that the purpose of the visioning process is to provide clear focus for the collective work of the faculty. A school that develops a school scenario for that purpose can have the document do double duty by turning it into an accountability device. This is done by having all stakeholder groups ratify the scenario. An annual endorsement by the site council, the school board, and the superintendent provides legitimacy to the claim that the pursuit of this statement is a top school priority. Once a scenario has become official policy, then holding people accountable to that vision becomes the primary business of the faculty.

Profiling Current Status

Chapter 13 also outlined a process for pulling achievement targets out of the school scenario and developing rating scales as evaluative criteria to assess performance on the targets. It is imperative that, for each target identified as a component of the schoolwide vision, a baseline of performance be established. Baselines are essential so that progress toward the target can be reliably documented. Many schools already prepare school report cards to distribute to their community. When developing a school report card, the most important data to provide are reports on progress on each of the school's priority achievement targets.

Commissioning or Conducting Action Research on Goal Areas

One of my favorite strategies for encouraging collaborative teacher inquiry is the establishment of a budget appropriated for action research and allocated at the discretion of the site council. The site council then uses this money to commission faculty action research on school priority areas. Site councils accomplish this in one of two ways. The council can issue requests for proposals (RFPs) on areas that the site council believes require more data to enable the faculty to advance on their targets. Another approach used in many schools is to ask teachers who desire support for their own action research projects to submit short proposals for financial support (as long as the projects are consistent with the school's vision).

Regardless of which approach is used, as the contracting agency, the site council stipulates that final payment is contingent on the submission of an acceptable research report to the council. Furthermore, the council may require a public report for others in the school community.

A school that uses this process will end each year with written reports containing the very type of data that accrediting agencies now ask for. Specifically, the school will be armed with reports on progress toward the achievement of priority school goals.

Generating a Composite Annual Report

Once the year's action research reports have been completed and submitted, then it becomes the job of either the site council or the administration to prepare a composite annual report. The final annual report has three generic components: an introduction, an action plan, and an appendix. Such an annual report might read like the sample shown in Figure 15.1.

A composite annual report like the one shown in Figure 15.1 could become the self-study that the school needs to submit as its part of the accreditation/program review process. If the review process involves a visitation from an external review team, the visiting team would then be asked to review the self-study (particularly the six action research reports), and to examine the data that informed those reports. Then, when conducting the visitation, the visiting team could discuss the appropriateness of the conclusions drawn and the action plans developed.

The four-step process outlined here is now accepted by all the major accrediting agencies in North America. Schools that have employed this process have found that accreditation no longer requires taking a break from other school improvement priorities. In fact, the self-study process of accreditation (when it consists of a set of focused collaborative action research projects) actually helps further the ongoing efforts and commitments of the faculty. As a final benefit, the report from the visiting team will provide the faculty with additional insights (and perhaps data) on topics they truly care about.

Some Final Thoughts

Perhaps nothing is as frustrating for today's classroom teacher as the seeming lack of coherence in school improvement initiatives. It often

FIGURE 15.1

A Sample Annual Report

Introduction

_____ Elementary School has committed itself to the realization of a shared vision that was approved by and is supported by the
Board of Education of _____ School District. Appendix A contains the full text of our vision, and Appendix B is the endorsement resolution
from the _____ Board of Education dated October 11, 1999.

The vision commits the professional staff of our school to the development of effective strategies to assist all of our students in meeting 27 specific
achievement targets at high levels of performance. The most recent assessment of our status regarding these 27 targets is included as Appendix C of
this report.

During the past school year the professional staff at _____
chose to invest in a study of our performance on six specific components of
our vision. The investigations conducted this year are listed below.

School Studies 1998–1999

I. The improvement of student writing through the "writing across the curriculum habit" (WATCH) program.

II. The development of student feelings of competence through attention
to multiple intelligences in lesson/unit planning.

III. The use of student self-assessment to build meta-cognitive skills.

IV. An investigation of the peer mediation program to determine whether
it is "problem-management competence."

V. A study of the "math in the real world" program to determine whether it
enhances problem-solving abilities.

VI. A study of how much long-term retention of skills occurs through "thematic instruction."

The following pages contain abstracts from those six Action Research
Reports that were conducted by a total of 23 _____ staff members. The
research reports themselves are Exhibits 1–6 in Appendix D.

Action Plan

Based upon the findings of this year's action research, the site council
has recommended the following actions for the next school year. These rec-
ommendations were ratified by the faculty with a 32-3 (91%) vote and unani-
mously by our Parent Advisory Council.

FIGURE 15.1—*continued*
A Sample Annual Report

Action Plan 1999–2000

A. We will continue our emphasis on thematic instruction while being more explicit about the transferable skills that we expect will be developed. We will explore ways to make planning for multiple intelligences an integral part of the thematic lesson planning process.

B. We will expand the "writing across the curriculum" project to include mathematics and the arts.

C. A student-faculty study group will examine ways to include self-assessment into our formal mechanisms for reporting of progress (conferences and report cards). We will conduct and evaluate field tests of these strategies.

D. We will find ways to continue to support and strengthen the peer mediation and "math in the real world" projects.

---

seems that teachers are serving multiple masters, each with differing agendas: parents, state departments of education, administrators, interest groups with special agendas, and so on, and so on. No wonder feelings of faculty efficacy are at an all time low in many schools. I have argued that the work lives of most teachers is the pursuit of passionate commitments continuously marked by "program interruptus!" In an organizational context that feels chaotic, teacher research appears to be just one more thing, piled on top of an already filled plate. In such cases, the prognosis for the survival of teacher research is remote at best.

If, however, school leaders want to make inquiry and action research an integral part of the fabric of everyday school life, it is imperative that they find every possible way to make school life and the school improvement process unified and coherent. The use of a collective vision to galvanize the direction of school improvement is one such technique. Freeing teachers to inquire into particular aspects of that vision that hold meaning for them is a great way to merge the teacher need for professional autonomy with leadership's legitimate desire to move the school in a clear direction. Finally, by making practical use of the data and the action research reports that were originally generated with the primary purpose of helping teachers grow or helping the school "learn its way forward" (for personnel evaluation or accreditation), leadership can help teachers gain satisfaction from their work without feeling overwhelmed by bureaucratic accountability.

Epilogue: Building a High-Efficacy Culture in Schools

To reduce the concept of organizational culture to the basics, we could say, "Culture is the way we do things here!" Patterns of behavior in any community are powerful. It becomes very hard, even risky, to stand against the prevailing pattern of behavior in any society or organization. Furthermore, it has been documented that, more often than not, culture is so powerful that culture changes people rather than the other way around. The main problem this book has tried to address is how to change the low professional efficacy of educators and in turn improve student performance. I firmly believe the root of the challenge is the prevailing organizational culture in many schools.

Prevailing Norms

In some schools, the culture, or "the way we do things here," involves a profound resistance to challenging old ideas on teaching, learning, and the nature of students. In some of these same venues, the organizational culture includes norms that support individualism over collective responsibility for the education of children. In such places "the way we do things here" implies "we won't share ideas, we won't criticize each other, and we won't otherwise interfere with each other's work."

In other schools, the prevailing norms couldn't be more different. In these "learning communities," the normal behavior is to share ideas, critique suggestions, visit each other's rooms, celebrate diversity, and wonder continuously, "What if . . .?" In these schools the values of the old African proverb "It takes a village to raise a child" become incorporated into a way of life. Observing life in these schools reveals a near constant dissatisfaction with the status quo, but the situation doesn't become a

202

source of despair, because there is shared confidence that collectively the members of the school community have the ability to do better tomorrow.

Sociologists tell us that every society or organization has a culture. In addition, we are told that cultures can differ in two important ways. First, cultures can be strong or weak. This means that the cultural norms, the patterns of "how we do things here," can either be adhered to by everyone, all of the time, with few if any exceptions, or they can be general patterns of behavior, often ignored without any apparent social sanction. Second, cultures can be either functional or dysfunctional. This means that cultural norms can either facilitate the society or organization in meeting its goals, or the norms and habits of "how we do things here" can interfere with the accomplishment of group goals.

These are concepts we all understand well when they are applied to the culture of the family. Some families have "tight cultures." They have rituals and traditions that are sacrosanct. Other families seem to have rules primarily so they can be broken. We all know families that function wonderfully. Members of these functional families support one another in the process of developing into self-actualized individuals. Positive ethical values are transmitted and reinforced through consistent behavior, and family life is enjoyed by everyone involved. Unfortunately, we also know of dysfunctional families in which patterns of behavior such as chemical abuse, violence, neglect, and the transmission of negative values work against achieving family goals of health and harmony.

Let's return to the issue that was the focus of this book—making schools productive and functional places for both teaching and learning. Every school has norms that facilitate accomplishing educational goals and norms that can seriously hinder a faculty's efforts to make their school a productive learning community for both students and teachers. In a marvelously titled article in *Educational Leadership*, "Good Seeds Grow in Strong Cultures," Jonathan Saphier and Matthew King (1985) reviewed the effective schooling literature and identified 12 norms that foster school improvement:

- Collegiality
- Experimentation
- High expectations
- Trust and confidence
- Tangible support
- Reaching out to the knowledge base
- Appreciation and recognition

- Caring, celebration, and humor
- Protection of what's important
- Involvement of stakeholders in decision making
- Traditions
- Honest, open communications

These norms are the markers of strong and functional school communities. The question remains: How do we transform a school culture that is currently dysfunctional into a strong and functional one? The research and experience of the Institute for the Study of Inquiry in Education suggests that this is done by first enunciating a set of core values and then providing the means for a professional to live and behave consistently in support of those values. Over time, engagement in work on core values can become the mechanism that can make cynical and frustrated teachers the caring and motivated people they were when they entered teaching.

Core Values

In the League of Professional Schools (Glickman, 1993), the school improvement process begins with the declaration of a "covenant" by the faculty. The covenant is a statement of the sacred purpose of the enterprise. Although it takes time to author a quality covenant, most schools can readily agree that their primary purpose is to assist students to achieve their maximal development through the acquisition of academic knowledge and skills. Furthermore, most would concur that this purpose is best accomplished through the work of the faculty. Therefore, it is imperative that we do everything in our power to develop and nurture top-quality faculties. The essential reason for enunciating core values is to clarify purposes. The rationale for supporting teachers is not primarily because we like them, but because good teachers are the means to a valued end—the education and empowerment of youth.

The conduct most critical to supporting a school's core values is the continuous and public behavior of *learning* by both students and adults. Whenever students or teachers are learning and growing, they are engaging in what schooling is all about. Even in the most negative school environments, opportunities can be created in which teachers and students can regularly share what they are learning.

If you find yourself in a negative environment, it is wise to create opportunities to share that do not involve captive (and occasionally hostile) audiences. Instead, set up voluntary meetings or study groups, providing attendees with credit, recognition, or food as incentives. These are wonderful contexts for voluntary sharing. I have observed schools where a small cadre of teachers doing action research have sustained themselves, adding members as they go. The longer this continues the deeper is the teachers' commitment to the belief that they can succeed in overcoming any curriculum, instructional, or organizational obstacles placed in their paths.

It is critical that all opportunities to share and learn be structured with open-admissions policies. Nothing is more counterproductive when trying to build a collegial culture than to have teacher research groups or inquiry groups become viewed as "elitist." For this reason, when you see others catching your enthusiasm, be prepared to welcome them into your circle with open arms.

School leaders need to seize every opportunity to expand the behaviors of action research into every aspect of school life. For example, they can share what they are learning about their own work through data and inquiry, using the inquiry process for schoolwide assessment (Chapter 15); validate inquiry by making it part of the evaluation process (Chapter 15); include it in staff development programs (Chapter 14); publicize the results of inquiry through newsletters and conferences (Chapter 13); use it to resolve disputes about pedagogical practices (Chapter 12); and use it to induct new members into the professional staff (Chapter 14). In addition, through both formal and informal mechanisms, leaders need to monitor the status of the school's culture across each of the 12 norms for productive work as outlined by Saphier and King.

In time, even in the worst of schools, a small cadre of inquiring educators engaged in behavior consistent with the school's core values can increase in number, resulting in a continued strengthening of the functional norms for a productive learning community. As these norms are strengthened, the fabric of the learning community is woven tighter and tighter and tighter!

Signs of Success

How do you know if it's working? Just listen. The best windows into a school's culture are the voices of the people working there. When you are in the faculty room, walking down the halls, or at a faculty party, are you hearing folks talk about their high expectations? Are they talking about the ideas they are intrigued with and trying out in their classrooms? Are they talking about what they are learning from student work products and other data on academic performance? If the answer is yes, you can be sure the norms of inquiry are in place and getting stronger.

Most important, when you see teachers (or students) regularly enunciating goals, following up with thoughtful theorizing on ways to accomplish those goals, implementing specific strategies consistent with their theories, and ultimately collecting and analyzing data on the effectiveness of their efforts, you will be witnessing a truly efficacious faculty.

As stated at the beginning of this book, many children are introduced at an early age to the story *The Little Engine That Could*. Perhaps the greatest gift we can give to our children is the opportunity to live and work during their school years in a community that pledges allegiance to the essential truth of that story every day and in every possible way.

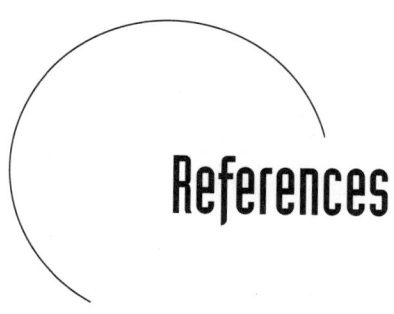

References

Bacharach, S. B., & Mundell, B. L. (1993). Organizational politics in schools: Micro, macro, and logics of action. *Educational Administration Quarterly, 29*(4), 423–452.

Brookover, W. B., & Lezotte, L. W. (1979). *Changes in school characteristics coincident with changes in student achievement.* East Lansing, MI: Michigan State University, College of Urban Development.

Bryk, A. S., & Driscoll, M. D. (1988, November). *The high school as community: Contextual influence and consequences for students and teachers.* Madison, WI: University of Wisconsin, National Center on Effective Secondary Schools.

Deming, W. E. (1986). *Out of crisis.* Cambridge, MA: MIT Center for Advanced Engineering Study.

Edmonds, R. (1979, October). Effective schools for the urban poor. *Educational Leadership, 37*(1), 15–24.

Fullan, M. G., & Stiegelbauer, S. (1991). *The new meaning of educational change.* New York: Teachers College Press.

Glickman, C. D. (1993). *Renewing America's schools: A guide for school-based action.* New York: Jossey-Bass.

Henstrand, J., & Johnson, D. G. (1993, Fall). Action research: Using student interviewers to link research and practice. *Teaching and Change, 1*(1), 29–44.

Holmes Group. (1990). *Tomorrow's schools: Principles for the design of professional development schools.* East Lansing, MI: The Holmes Group.

Hughes, A. T. (1992). *Teacher evaluation: An analysis of the implementation of a professional growth model.* Unpublished doctoral dissertation, Washington State University, Pullman.

Joyce, B., & Showers, B. (1982, October). The coaching of teaching. *Educational Leadership, 40*(1), 4-10.

Lerner, P., (1997). *Collaborative action research: Study guide.* Santa Monica, CA: Canter Educational Productions.

Levine, M., (1988). *Professional practice schools: Building a model.* Washington, DC: American Federation of Teachers.

Lightfoot, S. L. (1983). *The good high school: Portraits of character and culture.* New York: Basic Books.

Little, J. W. (1982). Norms of collegiality and experimentation: Workplace conditions of school success. *American Educational Research Journal, 19*(3), 325-340.

Miles, M. B., & Huberman, A. M. (1994). *Qualitative data analysis: An expanded sourcebook.* Thousand Oaks, CA: Sage.

Murphy, C. (1992, November). Study groups foster schoolwide learning. *Educational Leadership, 50*(3), 71–74.

Peters, T. J., & Waterman, R. H. (1982). *In search of excellence: Lessons from America's best-run companies.* New York: Harper and Row.

Reault, J. A. (1998). *Professionalism and growth-oriented teacher evaluation: A cross-case study of two school districts.* Unpublished doctoral dissertation, Washington State University, Pullman.

Robbins, P. (1991). *How to plan and implement a peer coaching program.* Alexandria, VA: ASCD.

Rosenholtz, S. J. (1989). *Teachers' workplace: The social organization of schools.* New York: Longman.

Rutter, M., Maughn, B., Mortimore, P., Ouston, J., & Smith, A. (1979). *Fifteen thousand hours: Secondary schools and their effects on children.* Cambridge, MA: Harvard University Press.

Sagor, R. D. (1981, December). A day in the life: A technique for assessing school climate and effectiveness. *Educational Leadership, 39*(2), 190–193.

Sagor, R. D. (1991, March). Collaborative action research: A report from Project LEARN. *Educational Leadership, 48*(6), 6–10.

Sagor, R. D. (1993). *How to conduct collaborative action research.* Alexandria, VA: ASCD.

Sagor, R. D. (1995, April). Overcoming the one solution syndrome. *Educational Leadership, 52*(7), 24–27.

Sagor, R. D. (1996). *Local control and accountability: How to get it, keep it, and improve school performance.* Thousand Oaks, CA: Corwin Press.

Sagor, R. D., & Barnett, B. G. (1994). *The TQE principal: A transformed leader.* Thousand Oaks, CA: Corwin Press.

Saphier, J., & King, M. (1985, March) Good seeds grow in strong cultures. *Educational Leadership, 42*(6), 67–73.

Sarason, S. B. (1982). *The culture of the school and the problem of change.* (2nd ed.). Boston: Allyn and Bacon.

Schein, E. H. (1992). *Organizational culture and leadership.* (2nd ed.). San Francisco: Jossey-Bass.

Senge, P. M. (1990). *The fifth discipline: The art and science of the learning organization.* New York: Doubleday.

Sergiovanni, T. J. (1992). *Moral leadership: Getting to the heart of school improvement.* San Francisco: Jossey-Bass.

Stiggins, R. J. (1994). *Student-centered classroom assessment.* New York: Merrill.

Veenman, S. (1984, Summer). Perceived problems of beginning teachers. *Review of Educational Research, 54*(2), 143–178.

Wagner, K. G. (1997). *Identification of the factors which significantly influenced the implementation of three team-taught multi-age programs.* Unpublished doctoral dissertation, Washington State University.

Index

About the Author

Richard Sagor took a leave from his position as an Associate Professor of Education at Washington State University in August of 1997 to found the Institute for the Study of Inquiry in Education, an organization committed to assisting schools and educators with their local school improvement initiatives. During the past decade Dick has facilitated workshops on the conduct of collaborative action research throughout the United States and internationally.

Dick has 17 years of experience in public schools, including work as a teacher, principal, and assistant superintendent. He is a frequent contributor to *Educational Leadership* and the author of the ASCD book *How to Conduct Collaborative Action Research*. Dick's other books include *At-Risk Students: Reaching and Teaching Them*, *The TQE Principal: A Transformed Leader*, and *Local Control and Accountability: How to Get It, Keep It, and Improve School Performance*.

He can be reached at the Institute for the Study of Inquiry in Education (ISIE), 602 NE 3rd Ave., Suite E-174, Camas, WA 98607. Phone: 360-834-3503. E-mail: rdsagor@isie.org.

Related ASCD Resources: Action Research

Audiotapes

Action Research: Easy Steps to Program Development and Assessment (live recording from the 1999 ASCD Annual Conference, #299068).

Curriculum Integration, Whole Language, and Teacher Action Research in an Urban Elementary School by Sharon Denero and Sherrie Gibney-Sherman (#61293159).

On Action Research (#295190) with Carl Glickman.

Results: The Essential Elements of Improvement with Mike Schmoker (#299335).

Using Data to Shape Classroom Practice by Richard DuFour (#299311).

Print Products

Creating Learning Experiences: The Role of Instructional Theory and Research by Bruce R. Joyce and Emily F. Calhoun (#196229).

How to Use Action Research in the Self-Renewing School by Emily F. Calhoun (#194030).

Real Questions, Real Answers: Focusing Teacher Leadership on School Improvement by John H. Clarke, Stephen D. Sanborn, Judith A. Aiken, Nancy A. Cornell, Jane Briody Goodman, and Karin K. Hess (#198007).

Research You Can Use to Improve Results by Kathleen Cotton, Northwest Regional Educational Laboratory (#399238).

Results: The Key to Continuous School Improvement, 2nd Edition, by Mike Schmoker (#199233).

Professional Inquiry Kit

Promoting Learning Through Student Data, developed by Marian Leibowitz (#999004).

Videotapes

Action Research: Inquiry, Reflection, and Decision Making (#495037). Featured Educators: Carl Glickman and Emily Calhoun.

ASCD product numbers for the above products are noted in parentheses. For additional resources, visit us on the World Wide Web (http://www.ascd.org), send an e-mail message to member@ascd.org, call the ASCD Service Center (1-800-933-ASCD or 703-578-9600, then press 2), send a fax to 703-575-5400, or write to Information Services, ASCD, 1703 N. Beauregard St., Alexandria, VA 22311-1714 USA.